The Courtauld Collection

The Courtauld Collection

Masterpieces of Impressionism and Post-Impressionism

ART GALLERY OF ONTARIO

The Art Gallery of Ontario is funded by the people of Ontario through the Ministry of Citizenship, Culture, and Recreation. Additional operating support is received from the Municipality of Metropolitan Toronto, the Museums Assistance Program of the Department of Canadian Heritage, and The Canada Council.

This book is published on the occasion of *The Courtauld Collection*, the exhibition organized by the Art Gallery of Ontario, Toronto, and sponsored by Chrysler Canada Ltd. Special support provided by the Province of Ontario. Additional assistance provided by the Department of Canadian Heritage.

Canadian Cataloguing in Publication Data
Courtauld Institute Galleries
      The Courtauld Collection

Catalogue essays by Maxwell L. Anderson and others.
Catalogue of an exhibition held at the Art Gallery of Ontario, June 10 – Sept. 20, 1998
Includes bibliographical references and index.
ISBN: 1-895235-87-1

1. Impressionism (Art) – France – Exhibitions. 2. Post-Impressionism (Art) – France – Exhibitions. 3. Painting, French – Exhibitions. 4. Painting, Modern – 19th century – France – Exhibitions. 5. Painting, Modern – 20th century – France – Exhibitions. 6. Courtauld Samuel, 1876–1947 – Art collections – Exhibitions. 7. Courtauld Institute Galleries – Exhibitions. I. Anderson, Maxwell Lincoln. II. Art Gallery of Ontario. III. Title.

ND547.5.I4C68 1998   759.4′074′713541   C98-931214–3

Many of the entries in this catalogue are based on texts by John House which appear in *Impressionism for England: Samuel Courtauld as Patron and Collector*, London, 1994, where further references can be found.

Authors:
Alan Chong: A.C.
Martha Kelleher: M.K.
Michael Parke-Taylor: M.P.T.
David Wistow: D.W.

Front cover: Édouard Manet, *A Bar at the Folies-Bergère*, detail, cat. 14
Inside front cover: Edgar Degas, *After the Bath, Woman Drying Herself*, detail, cat. 20
Back cover: Paul Gauguin, *The Haystacks*, detail, cat. 45
Inside back cover: Pierre-Auguste Renoir, *La Loge*, detail, cat. 30
Pages 2–3: Paul Cézanne, *Mont Sainte-Victoire*, detail, cat. 37
Pages 4–5: Edgar Degas, *Ballet Scene*, detail, cat. 16
Page 10: Vincent van Gogh, *The Crau at Arles: Peach Trees in Flower*, detail, cat. 49
Page 12: Paul Cézanne, *Tall Trees at the Jas de Bouffan*, detail, cat. 33
Page 14: Camille Pissarro, *Lordship Lane Station, Dulwich*, detail, cat. 24

Contents

Directors' Foreword

SERENDIPITY PLAYS AN ESSENTIAL ROLE in mounting museum exhibitions. The undersigned came together in 1997 to explore the possibility of bringing the great Impressionist and Post-Impressionist collections of the Courtauld Institute of Art to Toronto, North America's fifth largest city. The collegial spirit that informed the decision rests on the many points of contact between our two institutions. These range from alumni and alumnae of the Courtauld's renowned graduate program in the history of art, to many shared interests in scholarship, presentation, and new forms of communication just emerging in the museum landscape.

There are many to thank for this transatlantic collaboration. At the Courtauld Institute, we must single out Christine Butterfield who worked collaboratively with the Art Gallery of Ontario to facilitate this ambitious project. Linda Milrod was the project director at the Art Gallery of Ontario. She worked with Alan Chong, curator of European art, and many colleagues from the gallery to bring this exhibition to enthusiastic Toronto audiences.

The exhibition of masterworks from the Courtauld Collection is generously sponsored by Chrysler Canada Ltd. We thank them for their support and partnership. Our special international partner on this project is *Apollo* magazine, London.

The Province of Ontario recognized immediately the significance of this undertaking and provided the marketing support required to make this project a cultural and tourism success. We would also like to thank the Department of Canadian Heritage for their assistance with insuring the works of art while in Canada.

In closing, we appreciate the brisk and determined pace of our respective staffs in preparing and mounting the exhibition for its trip to Toronto and display here. We hope that it will inspire generations of museum visitors to return to The Strand in London to enjoy these and other works which comprise the remarkable collection of the Courtauld Institute of Art.

Maxwell L. Anderson
DIRECTOR
ART GALLERY OF ONTARIO
TORONTO

John Murdoch
DIRECTOR
COURTAULD GALLERY
COURTAULD INSTITUTE OF ART
LONDON

Sponsor's Foreword

CHRYSLER CANADA LTD., IS PLEASED to sponsor *The Courtauld Collection* at the Art Gallery of Ontario. Our involvement is consistent with our philosophy that corporate success must be complemented with corporate responsibility. Throughout our history, Chrysler Canada has sought to fulfil that responsibility by providing assistance to organizations that share our vision for a better Canada. We believe that this once-in-a-lifetime exhibition will enrich the lives of tens of thousands of Canadians.

There was never a greater champion of the preservation and enhancement of our country than our recently deceased chairman, president, and C.E.O., Mr. G. Yves Landry. His passion for Canada ranged from our initiatives in education to ensure preparedness of our youth for meaningful, worthwhile employment, through support of our Olympic athletes, to the vision of the Trans Canada Trail.

Mr. Landry's legacy is perhaps best summarized by his often quoted statement:

"We're not just building cars and trucks. We're building Canada."

Chrysler Canada and its employees are proud to dedicate the sponsorship of *The Courtauld Collection* to the memory of G. Yves Landry, O.C.

William Glaub
PRESIDENT AND CHIEF EXECUTIVE OFFICER
CHRYSLER CANADA LTD.

The Courtauld Collection at the Art Gallery of Ontario

FOR MANY, THE ART OF THE IMPRESSIONISTS and Post-Impressionists hold magical sway. Their work today connotes a painterly style that rewards easily through a sensuous, sun-dappled palette and a deceptively playful technique in brushwork. That now-beloved technique was, ironically, ridiculed and despised in its time as an abnegation of the achievements of Western art from Raphael onwards, while today it exercises an undeniable allure. Yet technique alone cannot explain the formidable magnetism of works bearing the adjective "impressionist." Instead, it is a combination of features which drives millions into special exhibitions each year, seeking a visceral connection with those painters whose names are the gold standard of museums.

To begin with, the subjects of the Impressionists marked a departure from the prevailing fare of academic and romantic painters. Rather than obscure Old Testament and classical allegories, windswept heroes of legends past, or sombre magnates posing for portraits, the Impressionists turned to unpretentious scenes of contemporary life. They eschewed the confines of the studio for the rough and tumble of a new industrial age, caught in the sunlight, and prettified it. Powerful trains and wrought-iron suspension bridges were novel fare, and the pastoral landscapes of France had yet to be scarred by the impact of industry's manifest destiny. The soft-focus lens of the Impressionist palette makes every woman a great beauty, every landscape an Eden, every monument timeless, and every city cleansed of the cares of pollution, noise, and poverty. The appeal is undiminished to this day.

The general public has to work harder, as do art historians, to interpret the religious, historical, biblical, or mythological subjects that dominated the history of art in the centuries from the fall of the Roman Empire up until these unlikely protagonists emerged. The Impressionist painters found their inspiration in the present. And just as the average museumgoer (there being no such person) would likely prefer not to have their knowledge tested on a day off to study Pre-Raphaelite painting, they may find the emergence of non-objective painting in the early twentieth century to be no more inviting.

Impressionist paintings spanning from the 1870s by Pissarro to the late Monets of the 1920s provide a respite from the historically referential body of art history before them as well as from the cerebral achievements of Malevich and his contemporaries.

Whereas the general public makes no effort to conceal its devotion to Monet and his contemporaries, for most scholars, the terms "Impressionism" and "Post-Impressionism" have become a straitjacket. There are great artists like Manet who fit awkwardly into such categories and there are significant contemporary achievements in nineteenth-century art which are overlooked because of the overwhelming adulation of those artists who may fairly be associated with these two movements. Like Canada's Group of Seven, these French artists, rejected by the academic salon and loosely organized, were to varying degrees calculating in striking a revolutionary posture that would later forge their successful public profile. Once spurned, they organized their own exhibitions outside the Academy and created a sensation.

More recently, scholars have sought to interpret the works of Impressionist painters from new vantage points, informed by the political subtexts of Pissarro's works or the alleged misogynism of Degas. These historians ply their trade to deaf ears in the general public, whose love affair with the artists is so inflamed as to reject any intimations of their infidelity to the cause of *ars gratia artis*, or art for art's sake.

The works in the present exhibition from the Courtauld Institute of Art are exceptional in two respects: they are uniformly of the highest quality, and they include some of the icons of nineteenth-century art. The cover image of this catalogue, *A Bar at the Folies-Bergère*, is one of the most celebrated images in the history of art, and may be singled out as one of the exhibition's greatest rewards. It is among the most thoroughly documented paintings in art historical scholarship. Much research has focused on the social subtext of the scene and its protagonist. The bar girl has a gaze no less timeless than that of the Mona Lisa, and just as inscrutable. The mirror behind her reflects our own voyeurism. While from the front she appears to be standing erect, the reflection of her back suggests that she leans forward towards the man who looms close to the barmaid, as if entertaining his proposition.

This one painting has an enormous amount to tell us about life in nineteenth-century Paris and the artistic tensions that to a large extent defined it; the balance of the exhibition is no less articulate. From the landscapes and still lifes of Cézanne to the beachside genre scenes of Boudin, urban interiors of Degas, a pastoral rhapsody by Gauguin, a classicizing allegory by Manet, documentary panoramas of Pissarro, and dozens of other records of the vision of that century, no visitor to the exhibition will emerge without a deeply enriched appreciation of these inimitable chroniclers whom we have saddled with "isms" that are finally limiting stereotypes. Scholars today are reassessing the motivations and influences that combined to give birth to this movement, and do so from a variety of interpretive perspectives, ranging from the sociological to the post-structuralist. The presentation of great works in a fresh setting almost invariably gives rise to new insights, and such will, we trust, be the case in this display.

Great exhibitions perform no greater function than allowing us to reappraise what is before our eyes every day in museum collections around the world. The permanent collection of the Courtauld Institute is a testament to Samuel Courtauld's eye and his passion. Like other great collectors of his age and ours, he saw beyond the institutional vision of the Academy, or in our case, the museum. These are pictures of a scale appropriate to an opulent domestic setting, as Courtauld himself and his British and American competitors so ably demonstrated, rather than a cavernous institution created for public display. But their pilgrimage in exhibitions like this one serves to remind us of art history's endless cycles of taste and judgement, and of the tensions between the creative spirit and the stewards of that spirit. The reminder is both instructive about the art of our own time and, as in this case, adds yet more lustre to the achievements of those who worked in opposition to the received wisdom of the art establishment of late nineteenth-century Paris.

Maxwell L. Anderson
DIRECTOR
ART GALLERY OF ONTARIO

Samuel Courtauld and the Courtauld Institute of Art

Samuel Courtauld IV (fig. 1) was born in 1876 to a family of French Huguenot origin, and had been raised a Unitarian, a nonconformist and intellectual brand of Protestantism that had long been outside the mainstream of society in Britain. In the seventeenth century, the Courtaulds had settled in England as silversmiths, but by the early nineteenth century, the family was manufacturing silk in Essex. In the early 1900s, the family business acquired the patents for artificial silk, or rayon, and rapidly grew into a publicly held company of enormous size, with a large operating base in the United States. Samuel Courtauld was sent to study the silk business rather than to university, and became chairman of this incredibly profitable company in 1921.

What stimulated a wealthy industrialist with little exposure to art to suddenly embark on art collecting with such passion? Courtauld was curious about art, but it was not until he saw Hugh Lane's collection in 1917 that he became seriously interested in paintings:

> There I remember especially Renoir's *Parapluies* (fig. 14), Manet's *Musique des Tuileries* and Degas' *Plage à Trouville....* I knew nothing yet of Cézanne, but I was initiated in a curious way. A young friend of mine, who was a painter of conventional portraits, led me up to Cézanne's *Provençal Landscape* (fig. 2), belonging to Miss Davies, at an exhibition of the Burlington Fine Arts Club.... At that moment I felt the magic, and I have felt it in Cézanne's work ever since.[1]

Within the few short years between 1923 and 1929, Samuel Courtauld put together one of the most distinguished collections of Impressionist and Post-Impressionist paintings.

---

1. From unpublished memoirs of Samuel Courtauld, quoted by Anthony Blunt, "Samuel Courtauld as Collector and Benefactor" in Douglas Cooper, *The Courtauld Collection: A Catalogue and Introduction*, London, 1954, pp. 3–4.

Fig. 1. Samuel Courtauld, photograph, July 1936.

Fig. 2. Cézanne, *Mountains in Provence*, around 1879, National Museums and Galleries of Wales, Cardiff. Acquired by Gwendoline Davies in 1918, this work marked a turning point in Samuel Courtauld's appreciation of Cézanne.

The Courtauld Institute of Art is both a school devoted to art history as well as a public art gallery. An integral part of the University of London, the institute was founded in 1931 principally on the initiative of Viscount Lee of Fareham (1868–1947) with the financial backing of Samuel Courtauld (1876–1947). The notion that an important university should teach the history of art as well as collect art sprang not from the venerable British universities such as Cambridge and Oxford, which, although they possessed great museums, did not formally teach art history, but from American colleges like Harvard and Yale which already in the 1800s had integrated the teaching of art history with an art collection. Using Harvard's Fogg Art Museum as his model, Lord Lee approached the University of London in 1928 with a plan to establish a professional school of art history. Samuel Courtauld generously committed £100,000 to the project, and set up an additional endowment. After the death of his wife Elizabeth in 1931, Courtauld decided to vacate his house on Portman Square so that the new institute could have a home. The Courtauld Institute soon attracted other backers who supported the library, photographic archives, and a department of technology.

Samuel Courtauld also gave many of his nineteenth-century French pictures to the institute which bore his name and, at his death in 1947, bequeathed nearly all of his collection, since it had been his intention that students should study near major works of art. Unfortunately the elegant rooms of his house soon became inadequate for a growing institute. In 1958, the art collection was installed in separate Courtauld Institute Galleries, a small exhibition space on the fifth floor of a building in Bloomsbury. In 1990, all of the facilities of the Courtauld Institute, including classrooms, libraries, offices, as well as galleries, were relocated to Somerset House (fig. 3), bringing together once again the teaching of art history and a major art collection. A.C.

Fig. 3. Somerset House, designed by
Sir William Chambers, around 1776–1780.

Honoré Daumier
Marseilles 1808–1879 Valmondois

[1]

HONORÉ DAUMIER

The Defence 1860s

pencil, pen and ink, and wash on paper, 23.7 x 31.5 cm
signed lower right: h. D.
HISTORY: Bought by Samuel Courtauld in 1928 from the
Independent Gallery, London. Courtauld Bequest 1948.

[2]

HONORÉ DAUMIER

The Hypochondriac 1860s

black chalk and watercolour on paper, 20.7 x 27.1 cm
signed lower left: h / h. Daumier
HISTORY: Bought by Samuel Courtauld in 1929 from L'Art
Moderne, Lucerne. Courtauld Gift 1934.

[3]

HONORÉ DAUMIER
Don Quixote and Sancho Panza around 1870

oil on canvas, 100 x 81 cm
HISTORY: Ambroise Vollard, Paris, 1901. Paul Rosenberg, Paris
(1907, 1922). Galerie E. Bignou, Paris. Bought by Samuel Courtauld
in 1923 from L. H. Lefèvre and Son, London. Courtauld Gift 1932.

Daumier seems to have loved the tale of Don Quixote, possibly because of the satiric absurdity of the figure as presented by Cervantes. An early biographer of Daumier suggested that the artist saw aspects of himself both in the idealism of Don Quixote as well as in the peasant practicality of his companion Sancho Panza. In this painting, the two men ride side by side, Quixote astride a proud horse as Sancho Panza sits on an exhausted donkey. The work is essentially unfinished, the rapidly applied brown tones suggesting only the essential aspects of the figures and the deep valley.

The dark drama of this picture and its rough, unfinished brushwork had great appeal to twentieth-century observers. The undefined forms have been interpreted, however anachronistically, as modern in concept. In 1922, Roger Fry wrote of this "sketch" that it "gives once more a suggestion of what his tragic humour might have accomplished had he been able to work at painting with the continuity and persistence of a Rembrandt." Perhaps because of this response, Samuel Courtauld acquired the work the following year. A.C.

Constantin Guys
Vlissingen (the Netherlands) 1802–1892 Paris

[4]

CONSTANTIN GUYS

Two Women with Muffs around 1864

pencil, pen and brush in ink, and watercolour on paper
34.6 x 23.6 cm
HISTORY: Bought by Samuel Courtauld in 1928 from
Paul Rosenberg. Courtauld Gift 1938.

[5]

CONSTANTIN GUYS

A Woman of Easy Virtue around 1867–1870

pencil, black wash, with touches of watercolour, on paper
33.8 x 22.8 cm

HISTORY: Bought by Samuel Courtauld in 1928 from the
Leicester Galleries, London. Courtauld Bequest 1948.

Eugène Boudin
Honfleur 1824-1898 Deauville

[6]

EUGÈNE BOUDIN

Women on a Beach 1866

pencil and dilute gouache on blue paper, 10.4 x 16 cm
dated upper right: 1866; lower right: 66
studio sale stamp lower right: E B
HISTORY: Boudin studio sale, Paris, 1899. Bought by Sir Robert
Witt from Lefèvre, London. Witt Bequest 1952.

The concept of a fashionable seaside holiday became popular in the 1860s with the extension of railway lines from Paris to the seaside towns of Deauville, Trouville, and Le Havre, as well as the increase in the amount of leisure time available to the upper middle classes. Eugène Boudin was the artist principally responsible for making these new activities a subject in art. Although beach scenes had been painted by Dutch artists in the seventeenth century, Boudin, beginning in 1860, was the first to focus so intently on the social situations of the beach resort. A.C.

[7]

EUGÈNE BOUDIN
View of Antwerp Harbour,
with Sailing Vessels and Rowing Boat 1871

pencil and watercolour on paper, 12.7 x 21 cm
inscribed by the artist lower centre: matin
studio sale stamp lower right: E B
HISTORY: Boudin studio sale, Paris, 1899.
Acquired by Sir Robert Witt, London. Witt Bequest 1952.

[8]

EUGÈNE BOUDIN
Boats and Fisherfolk on the Beach, Berck 1880

pencil and dilute gouache on pale buff paper, 15.6 x 27.1 cm
inscribed upper left, above figures on the boat: Juin
studio sale stamp lower right: E B
HISTORY: Boudin studio sale, Paris, 1899. Sir Robert Witt.
Witt Bequest 1952.

[9]

EUGÈNE BOUDIN

Trouville 1875

oil on wood, 12.5 x 24.5 cm
signed lower left: Trouville E. Boudin
HISTORY: Louis de Wild, The Hague (auctioned in Paris, 1920).
M. Knoedler & Co., London and New York, 1925,
sold to Samuel Courtauld in 1926. Courtauld Gift 1932.

So much of Boudin's financial success depended on the happy, light-filled scenes of leisure on the beach. However, the artist was annoyed by their popularity and his dependence on them. As early as 1867, he complained of the empty fashionability of the seaside tourists:

The beach at Trouville, which a little while ago delighted us, looks on my return just like a terrible masquerade....

When you find yourself confronted with this troop of golden parasites who look so triumphant, it inspires a little pity in you and a certain shame in painting idle laziness. Fortunately, dear friend, the Creator spread a little of his splendid light everywhere and it is less these people than the element surrounding them which we are reproducing.

A.C.

[10]

EUGÈNE BOUDIN

Deauville 1893

oil on canvas, 50.8 x 74.2 cm

signed lower left: Deauville / E. Boudin 93

HISTORY: Dr. Delineau, Paris (auctioned 1901). Devilder, Roubaix.

Bought by Samuel Courtauld in 1936 from Wildenstein & Co.

Courtauld Bequest 1948 (on loan to R. A. Butler until 1983).

Boudin's late beach pictures do not capture the elegantly dressed holiday crowds depicted by Boudin early in his career (see cat. 9). The tiny figures seen in this painting are local fisherfolk with their carts and horses. Unlike the concentration on fashionable figures in the paintings of the 1860s, there is only a hint of a human presence as Boudin turns his attention to capturing the broad expanse of beach and sky. Monet, who greatly admired Boudin, remembered his advice, "Do as I did—learn to draw well and admire the sea, the light, the blue sky." With consummate skill Boudin depicts glowing skies, sparkling water, and the most subtle of changing weather conditions. M.K.

Édouard Manet
Paris 1832-1883 Paris

[11]
ÉDOUARD MANET
Le déjeuner sur l'herbe around 1867

oil on canvas, 89.5 x 116.5 cm
signed lower left: Manet
HISTORY: Given by Manet to Commandant Lejosne, Paris
(remaining in the family until 1924). Galerie Druet, Paris.
Bought by Samuel Courtauld in 1928 from the Independent Gallery,
London. Courtauld Gift 1932.

This painting is Manet's later version of *Le déjeuner sur l'herbe*, a work which has excited critical controversy since it was painted in 1863. Manet's picture (fig. 4), then titled "Le Bain" (Bathing), became the centre of an immense critical storm as even friendly critics objected both to the technique and subject. The image today remains enigmatic for many of the same reasons: why was a realistic, modern woman depicted naked next to clothed men?

Manet intended to rework Giorgione's *Concert champêtre* in the Louvre, which also shows nude nymphs with contemporaneously dressed males. Part of the appeal of Manet's work is that it is both homage to the old masters, as well as an ironic and comic updating.

It is important to distinguish between the celebrated original and Manet's later version, for the two are quite different not only in their historical position, but also in many aspects of their appearance. A remarkable work in itself, the Courtauld painting has attracted very little attention even in the nineteenth century. Although the Courtauld painting was once thought to be a preliminary oil sketch for the Paris version, it is almost certainly a later variation. X-radiographs show that the Paris version was altered and adjusted in numerous areas, as expected in the first version of a composition, while the Courtauld work shows almost no changes in the process of painting. The quick, broad handling also suggests that the Courtauld painting was made later in the 1860s.

The 1863 version seen in figure 4 is a very large work (208 x 264 cm) with life-size figures, while the Courtauld version is less than half of its size. Manet seems to have made this smaller canvas for a private collector. The two paintings have completely different purposes and audiences: the grand painting in Paris was meant for public display and to make a statement about Manet's artistic goals. The Courtauld work is essentially a private, domestic image.

Several adjustments have been made to the composition. The woman (modelled by Victorine Meurent) now has reddish hair, and the gesture of the man on the right (a figure based on Manet's brothers Eugène and Gustave)

Fig. 4. Manet, *Le déjeuner sur l'herbe*, 1863, Musée d'Orsay, Paris.

is set slightly differently. The man on the left (Ferdinand Leenhoff, the Dutch sculptor and Manet's brother-in-law) has a different expression. These refinements more tightly unify the group. Manet also more conventionally set the bathing woman in the distance.

One of the principal criticisms levelled at the original picture was the disparity of finish between the intensely modelled figures and the sketchy background. Théodore Pelloquet wrote in 1863:

> One can't really designate this product of Manet's labours as an *esquisse* [sketch] or an *ébauche* [preliminary study]. In an *esquisse* properly understood and properly executed, all the parts are rendered to the same degree. Nothing explains or justifies Manet's incoherence, his inequality of execution.[1]

Whether in response to such criticism or not, Manet's second version is more like a sketch. The original's unevenness has been entirely suppressed by an overall freedom and quickness of handling that binds the various parts of the composition together.

The sketchiness also reduces the sharp, incisive clarity of the woman's face. She no longer stares out so brazenly, nor is her nakedness set off in such strong relief. Now nude rather than naked, she is set on conventional drapery. The aggressive lighting, especially in the background, has also been filtered. Some of the most shocking features of the Paris version have therefore been nearly eliminated. In the Paris original, Manet audaciously fused several genres—portraiture, landscape, still life—which are here subsumed within a work which has the feeling of a compositional study.

Although it recalls a crucial image of Manet's early career, the spontaneity of the Courtauld's *Le déjeuner sur l'herbe* points towards the effects connected with Impressionism that Manet would strive for in the 1870s and early 1880s. A.C.

1. Théodore Pelloquet, *L'exposition: Journal du Salon de 1863*, 23 July 1863; quoted in Michael Fried, *Manet's Modernism*, Chicago, 1996, p. 305.

[12]

ÉDOUARD MANET

Woman at Her Toilet around 1860-1861

red chalk on paper, 29 x 20.8 cm
HISTORY: Marcel Guiot, Paris. Bought by Samuel Courtauld in 1928
from the Leicester Galleries, London. Courtauld Bequest 1948.

Manet did not leave a large corpus of drawings and is known today primarily as a painter. His earliest studies in pencil or chalk were copies after Renaissance and Baroque paintings. Although no direct source for *Woman at Her Toilet* has been established, the artist did make other, similar studies of nude women caught unawares which recall paintings of Susannah and the Elders or Bathsheba Bathing by Giulio Romano, Titian, Rembrandt, and Rubens.

The female nude was one of Manet's principal subjects in the late 1850s and early 1860s. In this drawing, the bathing woman clutches a robe to her chest as though she has just noticed a hidden observer. At the left, an attending handmaiden can be discerned. This voyeuristic theme is echoed in Manet's contemporary painting *The Surprised Nymph* (Museo Nacional de Bellas Artes, Buenos Aires).

The subject also anticipates the nude women in *Le déjeuner sur l'herbe* (cat. 11) which was titled "Le Bain" (Bathing) when the first version was exhibited in 1863.

Manet traced the lines of this drawing with a stylus to transfer the design to the copperplate from which the etching *La Toilette* was published in 1862 (fig. 5). In the print, a dark interior now envelops the figure, heightening the sense of a private space that has been invaded. Since many of Manet's early prints copy the subjects from his own paintings, the Courtauld drawing may represent an intermediate step between a painting that has been lost, or painted over, and the print. The horizontal lines that cross the knees of the bather in the drawing suggest that if a related painting once existed, Manet may have cropped or considered cropping his canvas. M.P.T.

Fig. 5. Manet, *La Toilette*, 1862 etching, Courtauld Gallery, London.

[13]

ÉDOUARD MANET

At the Ball around 1877

oil on canvas, 55.7 x 35.5 cm

HISTORY: Auctioned from the artist's estate, Paris, 1884. Acquired by
Count Antoine Seilern before 1960. Seilern Bequest 1978
(Princes Gate Collection).

ÉDOUARD MANET

A Bar at the Folies-Bergère 1881–1882

oil on canvas, 96 x 130 cm
signed lower left (on bottle): Manet / 1882
HISTORY: Manet estate sale, Paris, 1884, sold to Emmanuel Chabrier,
Paris (auctioned 1896, but failed to sell). Durand-Ruel, Paris, 1897.
Baron Ferenc Hatvány, Budapest, 1919. J. K. Thannhauser, Munich.
Eric Goeritz, Berlin. Bought by Samuel Courtauld in 1926 from
Thannhauser Gallery, Lucerne. Courtauld Gift 1934.

Manet's last major painting and one of art history's most famous images, *A Bar at the Folies-Bergère* has inspired countless interpretations and readings. Bars and cafés had been a popular subject for the Impressionists, and Manet himself had depicted the theme many times in the late 1870s (fig. 6). Unique to this work is the expanse of the scene shown in the mirror and, most especially, the compelling figure of the woman. She occupies the entire centre of the picture and looks out directly. Any understanding of *A Bar at the Folies-Bergère* rests ultimately on a personal reaction to the barmaid and what she represents. Who is she? What is suggested in her expression? Is she melancholic, overwhelmed, alluring, dazed, or simply bored and tired?

She is shown standing behind a marble bar, well stocked with champagne and Bass Ale, decorated with a small vase of roses and a bowl of oranges. The barmaid faces us directly, but her eyes seem to have wandered for a second, her face is perhaps tinged with sadness and exhaustion. Behind the bar is a complex scene shimmering with light and revellers. Two figures appear on the right: another waitress serving a customer? No, although the woman looks a little different from behind, this is apparently a reflection of the barmaid herself and a customer—the purported male viewer of the painting. Grand chandeliers and brilliant globe lights illuminate the scene but also create distortions and confusions in the vast mirror. Tucked into the upper left are two legs of a trapeze artist suspended high above the stage—a comic detail which

highlights the interiorized expression of the barmaid.

In 1882, the painting would have instantly triggered a whole set of associations and images for the contemporary viewer. The Folies-Bergère was a popular entertainment complex, part theatre, part café. Fashionable and expensive (unlike the typical *café-concert*), its multiple stages, lounges, and bars provided a notorious setting for elegant prostitutes, the Parisian *demi-monde*.

This background has led some writers to see the waitress as an occasional prostitute, and her expression as one of alienation and degradation. Others interpret her as a stoic observer of the pleasure for sale in the vast tumult glimpsed in the mirror. It is uncertain whether barmaids at the Folies-Bergère were actually available for sex. Manet's barmaid appears neither flirtatious nor promiscuous, but rather seems quiet and still, isolated from the noise and animation around her.

Manet had previously painted waitresses, for example, in a work of around 1878 (fig. 6), which was the first painting Samuel Courtauld purchased for the Tate Gallery in 1923. Courtauld deliberately selected two paintings by Manet with very similar themes. Here, too, a performance takes place on a stage in back, which, like the mirror in *A Bar at the Folies-Bergère*, represents a world isolated from the server.

The idea of a principal female figure who looks out directly at the viewer had earlier fascinated Manet in *Gare Saint-Lazare* (fig. 7). Compositionally the works are similar: a woman engages us directly while another figure

Fig. 6. Manet, *The Waitress (Corner in a Café-Concert)*, 1878–1879, National Gallery, London.

Fig. 7. Manet, *Gare Saint-Lazare*, 1873, National Gallery of Art, Washington.

turns away (the girl playing a role similar to the reflection). The fenced-off background, shrouded in steam, functions as a mysterious screen exactly as does the confused mirror in *A Bar at the Folies-Bergère*. In both works, Manet placed a large female figure very close to the picture plane, and set her against a backdrop that seemed flat but also provided glimpses of a space full of activity.

Manet asked one of the barmaids at the Folies-Bergère, a woman named Suzon, to pose for him. He made a preliminary oil sketch of the composition (fig. 8) which shows the model turned to the right while the customer is placed on a much lower level and wears a bowler hat. In some respects the oil sketch presents a more convincing reflection of the barmaid, but there remain points of confusion. X-radiographs show that Manet began the larger painting with an arrangement of figures close to the sketch in figure 8, but slowly and wilfully moved objects into their present position, possibly to create deliberate obfuscations, but certainly to enhance the composition.

At the Salon of 1882, contemporary viewers were disturbed by the apparent mistakes of the mirror's reflections. The bar and mirror do not appear to be parallel, and even if the mirror was assumed to be tilted, the reflections of the bottles do not correspond to those on the bar. Does it matter that the picture falls short of an empirical, photographic realism? The viewer is clearly invited to attempt to unravel the visual complexity of the painting, but the ambiguity of the perspective (and of the barmaid's reflection) must have been purposeful.

For centuries artists had been fascinated with mirrors, not only as interesting optical devices, but also as symbols of artistic vision. Manet deliberately positioned himself as successor to Parmigianino, van Eyck, and his beloved Velázquez, who all explored the mirror's effects. The significance of the mirror as an allegory for seeing and painting seems especially appropriate in this, Manet's last major picture. A.C.

Fig. 8. Manet, *Study for "A Bar at the Folies-Bergère,"* 1881.

36

Public and Private Collecting

Up until 1917, the National Gallery in London was not allowed to acquire works by living artists, while the Tate Gallery could only collect British works. Moreover, the trustees of the National Gallery seemed to have disliked Impressionism, refusing important gifts of works by Monet and Degas. This reaction is all the more shocking since such paintings were already common in museums and drawing rooms in the United States and Germany.

The National Gallery gradually changed its position, and began construction of a gallery for modern French pictures behind the Tate Gallery. In addition, Sir Hugh Lane's collection of pictures by Manet, Monet, Pissarro, Morisot, and Renoir (fig. 14) was bequeathed to the national museums. Furthermore, an independent and less conservative board of trustees was constituted for the Tate Gallery which began to purchase works by Gauguin, Degas, and Manet. This new attitude to Impressionism and Post-Impressionism set the stage for Samuel Courtauld's involvement.

In 1923, Samuel Courtauld presented the Tate Gallery with the sum of £50,000 to be used to acquire works of "the modern movement from its inception to the present time." Although the fund was legally administered by a committee of experts, in practice the purchase decisions were Courtauld's. Courtauld began to build his personal collection at the same time he made his monetary gift to the Tate and the two activities seem to have stimulated and cross-fertilized each other. In itself, this pattern is almost unique: no other major collector could have started from scratch, with almost no experience in the art market, to buy both for himself and for a major museum.

The Beginnings of the Collection

In September 1922, Samuel Courtauld bought his first French paintings[1]—a late painting by Renoir (cat. 32) and a work by Marchand of 1921 (cat. 77), acquired together for £1,750. The two works were of very recent making, and are the closest Courtauld would ever come to collecting contemporary painting. In the course of the following year, Courtauld's collecting quickly became more selective and ambitious as he acquired two paintings each by Gauguin, Cézanne, and Monet. The first works purchased for the Tate, Manet's *The Waitress* (fig. 6) and Renoir's *La première sortie* were several times more expensive than anything he had previously bought. In October 1923, Courtauld acquired an impressive landscape by Vincent van Gogh, *A Cornfield with Cypresses*, and a few months later, Van Gogh's sister-in-law was persuaded to sell the artist's *Sunflowers* and *Chair and Pipe*, even though she had initially resisted offers. The Tate Gallery now had three important works, of different subjects, by Van Gogh. Only a month later, perhaps the most remarkable painting of the gift, Seurat's *Une baignade, Asnières* (fig. 9) was bought for £3,900. Thus by 1925, important masterpieces had been acquired for the national collection, but comparatively little for Courtauld's private collection. This quickly changed as Cézanne's *Mont Sainte-Victoire*, Renoir's *La Loge* (cat. 30), and Manet's *A Bar at the Folies-Bergère* (cat. 14) were purchased in the space of a year.

Most of the Courtauld Gift was exhibited in the Tate Gallery in 1926 to popular and critical approval, both of the quality of the works and of Courtauld's generosity.

Fig. 9. Seurat, *Une baignade, Asnières*, 1883–1884, National Gallery, London.

The Separation of the Two Collections

Courtauld's collecting patterns suggest that the public gifts and the private collections were conceived at least initially as a unit, and there was hope that the two sections would be eventually reunited. His decision in 1932 to start giving his paintings to the newly constituted Courtauld Institute of Art must have been quite a shock to the board of the Tate Gallery who clearly expected an eventual bequest of at least some of the paintings.

Although we have no information regarding Courtauld's thinking at the time, Lord Lee seems to have been instrumental in convincing Samuel Courtauld that his collection belonged in the new educational institution. Perhaps the example of Harvard University's Fogg Art Museum which combined teaching with collecting functions was persuasive in itself. The exciting new mission of the Courtauld Institute must have appealed to Courtauld's sense of public service, and may have been enough to dissolve the ties with the Tate and National galleries.

Ironically, Lord Lee was also chairman of the National Gallery, which represented a conflict of interest, although this was not publicly discussed at the time. Kenneth Clark, director of the National Gallery, later recalled:

> I cannot help thinking that if [Courtauld's pictures] had been in the National Gallery they would have achieved more fully Mr. Courtauld's express wish that the art of the period should be widely appreciated. He changed his mind under pressure from Lord Lee, who wanted his own collection to be kept together in a private gallery and rightly believed that it would not be accepted unless it could be made part of a package deal with the Courtauld pictures.[2]

Soon after, Samuel Courtauld himself became chairman of the National Gallery's board, and placed on loan there his three most important paintings, Cézanne's *Mont Sainte-Victoire*, Renoir's *La Loge* (fig. 10), and Manet's *A Bar at the Folies-Bergère*. Although these works were legally the property of the University of London, it was thought that somehow this could be altered. However, in 1955 the Courtauld Institute set up its own gallery for the display of its collection. A.C.

---

1. In 1921, he bought two portraits by Thomas Gainsborough which had once belonged to his mother's family.

2. Kenneth Clark, *Another Part of the Wood: A Self-Portrait*, London, 1974, p. 265.

Fig. 10. Dining room, Home House, London, showing Renoir's *La Loge* (cat. 30).

Edgar Degas
Paris 1834-1917 Paris

[15]

EDGAR DEGAS

Woman at a Window around 1871-1872

essence on paper, 61.3 x 45.9 cm
signed lower right: Degas
stamped lower right: Degas
HISTORY: Alex. Reid, Glasgow (auctioned in Paris, 1898).
Durand-Ruel, Paris, sold around 1901 to Walter Sickert for his former
wife Ellen Cobden. Bought by Samuel Courtauld in 1927 from
the Leicester Galleries, London. Courtauld Gift 1932.

Like fellow Impressionist painters Renoir and Monet, Degas was fascinated by effects of light, but unlike his friends, he consistently studied light in interior spaces rather than out of doors. In this painting the light emanates from a tall, typically Parisian window, although it remains unclear whether the bold patch of white pigment is a blind or the sky cut by distant rooftops. The artist appears to have delighted in such ambiguities. Against this bright backdrop the figure is sharply silhouetted like an Egyptian relief, her face cast in deep shadow. The painting is Degas' record of an "accident," an unplanned, unposed moment when the human body, under certain conditions, seems to flatten mysteriously and dematerialize. The painting is clearly not a portrait, since the figure seems little more than an excuse for studying such extreme effects of light and shadow.

Using essentially only black and white, but exploiting the warm buff tone of the paper, Degas rapidly laid in broad areas of pigment, offset by a few passages of intense, even nervous, brushwork, visible, for example, in the woman's hair ornament. By using quick-drying essence, or *peinture à l'essence* (oil pigments drained of their oil medium and then diluted with turpentine or gasoline), he could work with great speed over the paper's surface, creating thin washes not unlike watercolour. By the standards of its day, the painting was considered unfinished, yet how forcefully it seizes a moment from the flux of time. D.W.

EDGAR DEGAS
Ballet Scene 1874

oil on canvas, 61.5 x 46 cm
signed lower left: Degas
HISTORY: Exhibited in London, 1874, when bought by Henry Hill,
Brighton (auctioned 1889), bought by Goupil with Victor Desfossés,
sold in 1899 to Paul Gallimard, Paris. Alex. Reid, Glasgow.
Sir James Murray, Aberdeen (auctioned 1927).
Bought by Samuel Courtauld in 1927 from M. Knoedler & Co.
Courtauld Gift 1932.

For Degas, ballet was an obsession. It inspired the greater part of his art, including over fifteen hundred paintings, pastels, prints, sculptures, and even fan decorations. Over the years experts have speculated about the origins of this lifelong fascination. Certainly Degas' family, especially his father, was musically inclined, and the artist's earliest depictions of ballet performances focused on the orchestra players and omitted all but the dancers' legs and lower torsos. Degas himself spoke of a fascination with body movement and pretty materials. Yet his regular attendance at ballet classes, rehearsals, and performances — he apparently attended performances three times weekly — aroused a deep admiration for the regimen which ballet demands. Similar principles lay at the core of his own artistic labours. Note the attention he pays to the foreground dancer's pronounced calf muscles, developed through years of training. Surely, too, Degas recognized in the illusionism of performance his own search for ways to recreate reality. But it may ultimately have been the dancer's endless pursuit of the ideal line — the exact placement of all parts of the body according to a centuries-old tradition — that resonated most deeply within Degas. Drawing lay at the core of his art and his draughtsmanship remained unequalled during his lifetime. Certainly until old age and near blindness, he saw contour lines as powerful expressive tools. The foreground dancer's elegant left arm, for example, with its silhouette sharply accented by stage lights, seems to wed the dancer's and painter's quest for the perfect line.

Like his contemporaries Monet and Renoir, Degas sought to express the fugitive quality of life around him. In this painting he not only arrests the lyrical movements of the performance, he employs witty compositional devices — the expanse of bare floor and the dancer daringly sliced by the left edge of the picture — to convey the candid, seemingly arbitrary, nature of the image. Yet the creative process itself was long and arduous. The artist usually produced rapid drawings in the classroom and then posed dancers in his studio. From these varied experiences (including the memory of performances) Degas constructed the final snapshot-like picture. He himself saw the irony in this. "No art," he said, "is less spontaneous than mine."

In the same year this work was painted, Degas used the two dancers in a multi-figured painting done in monochrome (fig. 11) which was exhibited in the first Impressionist exhibition of 1874. In the Courtauld painting, the dancers are further distanced and the scene is no longer a rehearsal. The privileged vantage point of the viewer from the box of honour near the stage, which might have been available to anyone in a rehearsal, now suggests a rich spectator of considerable status. D.W.

Fig. 11. Degas, *Ballet Rehearsal on Stage*, 1874, Musée d'Orsay, Paris.

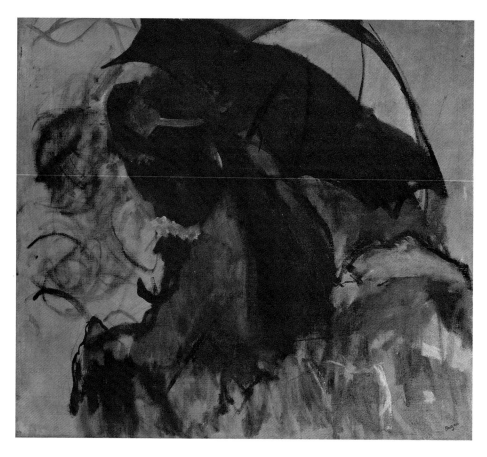

[17]

EDGAR DEGAS

Lady with a Parasol around 1877

oil on canvas, 75.3 x 85 cm
studio sale stamp lower right: Degas
HISTORY: Degas studio auction, Paris, 1918. Marcel Guérin, Paris
(1923, 1931). Bought by Count Antoine Seilern in 1954 in Paris.
Seilern Bequest 1978 (Princes Gate Collection).

Lady with a Parasol is comparable to *Woman at a Window* (cat. 15) in two ways: both show a figure seen against the light, and both were left unfinished; *Lady with a Parasol* remained in Degas' studio until his death. In both, too, certain parts are treated with great delicacy—here, the woman's profile and hat—in contrast to the breadth and summariness of the rest.

There is no clear indication in this work of the setting in which the figure is placed. However, an old label on the picture named it "At the Racecourse" (Aux courses), and another painting of a very similar profiled figure includes a racecourse in the background. *Lady with a Parasol* seems to belong to the large group of works that Degas made between the late 1860s and early 1880s which deal with horse racing, and particularly with the relationship between the spectators and the races; this was part of his wider interest in the most characteristic scenes of modern life. Often in these scenes the spectators show little interest in the spectacle, and here the downturned head of the woman suggests that she is absorbed in thought or conversation, and ignores whatever is going on beyond her.

[18]

EDGAR DEGAS

A Dancer around 1878

oil on silk, 23.5 x 13.5 cm
signed lower centre: Degas
HISTORY: Percy Moore Turner, London. Sir Kenneth Clark,
sold in 1941 to Count Antoine Seilern. Seilern Bequest 1978
(Princes Gate Collection).

[19]

EDGAR DEGAS

Seated Woman Adjusting Her Hair around 1884

charcoal, chalk, and pastel on paper, 63 x 59.9 cm
studio sale stamp lower right: Degas
HISTORY: Degas studio auction, Paris, 1918. Nunès et Fiquet, Paris.
Bought by Samuel Courtauld in 1923 from the Leicester Galleries,
London. Courtauld Bequest 1948.

What a common occurrence this image records! Fashion in the late nineteenth century dictated that women wear their long hair pinned up. Women washing, combing, or adjusting their hair inspired some of Degas' finest paintings, drawings, prints, and sculptures, and he keenly observed the actions of the body as these rituals were performed. Like so much of his art, this drawing extracts from a flow of movements a telling moment as the sitter leans forward, twists slightly to the left, and raises both hands to her head.

It was the realm of the everyday—rather than the world of the imagination—that captivated Degas and earned him a place amongst the Parisian avant-garde. Above all he depicted what was unabashedly modern, ordinary as one contemporary critic put it, "It is necessary to have genius to set down simply and surely what one sees before one's eyes."

This work is essentially two drawings on top of each other, for Degas reworked an earlier image. The ghost of the first drawing is still visible, especially along the curve of the model's back and hip, and clearly Degas was required to add a section of paper to the top to accommodate his expanded concept. D.W.

[20]

EDGAR DEGAS

After the Bath, Woman Drying Herself around 1895–1900

pastel on paper, 67.7 x 57.8 cm
studio sale stamp lower left: Degas
HISTORY: Degas studio sale, Paris, 1918. Trotti, Paris. Winkel &
Magnussen, Copenhagen, 1920. Lord Ivor Spencer-Churchill,
London. Bought by Samuel Courtauld in 1929 from the Independent
Gallery, London. Courtauld Gift 1932.

Beginning in 1880, Degas made a large number of pictures showing women bathing. Degas described his intention to depict "a human creature preoccupied with herself— a cat who licks herself" and to study these activities unnoticed "as if you looked through a key-hole." A group of the bathing pictures was shown in the 1886 Impressionist exhibition where they attracted much attention. Many critics attacked the paintings for many of the same reasons modern viewers find them disturbing. The works seemed to depersonalize the women depicted, the point of view appeared voyeuristic, and Degas was labelled a misogynist. Degas himself confessed, "Perhaps I looked on women too much as animals."

Despite adverse reaction, Degas continued to explore the theme of bathing women in the 1890s and early years of the twentieth century. These later bathing pictures, of which *After the Bath, Woman Drying Herself* is an example, differ from the works of the 1880s in their being more brilliantly coloured and richly textured. Degas made more than two hundred pastels of bathers, and even the oil paintings of this subject (fig. 12) echo the electric shimmer of the pastels.

Many commentators have found multiple layers of meaning in Degas' later bathing pictures, especially since the figures seem so vivid and powerful. Awkward yet muscular, the woman depicted here is immensely compelling. She concentrates on vigorously drying herself with a towel, evincing the concentration and self-absorption which Degas strove to capture. The athletic poses of Degas bathing women sometimes resemble academic studies of the male nude. The gesture of the raised arm could almost be a traditional gesture with a posing rope, while the dark outlines and aggressive shading further suggest strength and masculinity. Degas made numerous charcoal drawings and pastels of this particular composition, and even produced a sculpture in brown wax that may have served as a model (fig. 13). He claimed to be developing a new method of depicting the nude, but the pose and the working method suggest a considerable debt to the academic tradition. Just as the position of the woman suggests an awkward struggle, so the application of pastel is aggressive and tense. A.C.

Fig. 12. Degas, *Woman at Her Bath*, around 1895, oil on canvas, Art Gallery of Ontario, Toronto.

Fig. 13. Degas, *Seated Woman Drying Herself*, brown wax, National Gallery of Art, Washington.

[21]

CLAUDE MONET
Autumn Effect at Argenteuil 1873
oil on canvas, 55 x 74.5 cm
signed lower right: Claude Monet / 73
HISTORY: Durand-Ruel, Paris (perhaps exhibited in 1876); exhibited
in London in 1883 at Dowdeswell as "Le petit bras à Argenteuil."
Erwin Davis, New York, 1886. Durand-Ruel, 1901.
G. Hoentschel, Paris, 1904. Comte de Rasti, Paris. Alexandre
Rosenberg, Paris. Bought by Samuel Courtauld in 1924 from Galerie
Bernheim-Jeune, Paris. Courtauld Gift 1932.

This quiet tributary of the Seine meets the main river just southwest of Argenteuil, a town nine kilometres north of Paris where Monet lived from 1871 to 1878. Engulfed in brilliant autumn foliage, the Île Marante is seen on the left while the town of Argenteuil itself, with its church spire, appears in the distance. The darker blue water just before the town is the Seine.

Monet filled some 175 canvases with the various suburban activities of Argenteuil, which was rapidly growing. While he often depicted Argenteuil's railway line, industrial activities, and, most frequently, pleasure boating, here there is almost no sign of the modern world. This simple, classical composition focuses on the reflections in the river and the interactions between oranges and blues.

Indeed, the arrangement of the picture has a rigorous symmetry that is unusual in Monet's work.

Painted in the year before the first Impressionist exhibition, *Autumn Effect at Argenteuil* was exhibited extensively in Monet's lifetime. It made an early appearance in London in 1883. Frederick Wedmore described the painting's "palpitating light and glowing hue. The whole of one side of the canvas is filled with flame-coloured autumn trees which throw their bright reflections of a rosier flame-colour upon a broad river-water otherwise turquoise and opal."[1] A.C.

1. "The Impressionists," *Fortnightly Review*, January 1883, p. 82. Quoted by John House, *Impressionism for England: Samuel Courtauld as Patron and Collector*, London, 1994, p. 118.

[22]

CLAUDE MONET
Vase of Flowers around 1881–1882

oil on canvas, 100.4 x 81.8 cm
signed lower right: Claude Monet
HISTORY: Bought by Samuel Courtauld in 1923 from Alex. Reid,
Glasgow. Courtauld Gift 1932.

CLAUDE MONET
Antibes 1888

oil on canvas, 65.5 x 92.4 cm
signed lower left: Claude Monet 88
HISTORY: Probably exhibited in 1888 at Boussod, Valadon, Paris
(organized by Theo van Gogh). Exhibited in 1889 at
Georges Petit, Paris. Mme Barbedienne, Paris (auctioned 1894),
bought by Durand-Ruel. Edmond Decap, Paris, 1894.
Bernheim-Jeune, Paris, 1907. Bruno Caccamisi, Paris, 1907.
Mrs. Blanche Marchesi, London, around 1910. Paul Rosenberg, Paris.
Bought by Samuel Courtauld in 1923 from M. Knoedler & Co.,
London; to Sir John Atkins, London (life interest), to the
Courtauld Institute of Art in 1962.

In 1884 and 1888, Monet wintered on the Mediterranean coast to search for new subjects and different light effects. He lived in Antibes between February and May of 1888, working diligently to complete thirty-nine canvases. Rich and strong in colour, these paintings confused many critics and have been largely ignored by later art historians. Only recently have the landscapes come to be more widely appreciated and it is quite remarkable that Samuel Courtauld chose to purchase such an unusual work in 1923 as one of his three representative paintings by Monet.

This strikingly beautiful painting shows a single pine tree set against a brilliant blue sea, the Estérel mountains forming a screen across the back. The simple banded composition allows the brilliant colour to evoke southern sunshine and warmth. The heightened palette is remarkably different from Monet's northern landscapes. He wrote to Alice Hoschedé (whom he had been living with since 1878 and would marry in 1892), "What I will bring back from here will be pure, gentle sweetness: some white, some pink, and some blue, and all this surrounded by the fairylike air."[1]

The foliage of the pine tree skims the profile of the distant mountain range, an effect enhanced by Monet's repeating brushstrokes which can be compared with Cézanne's *Mont Sainte-Victoire* (cat. 37) made about the same time. Monet's picture belongs to a set of seven canvases depicting trees along a shore. Joachim Pissarro likens the arrangement of this group to the rhythm of a sonnet. This series paved the way for Monet's working method in the 1890s when he turned his attention to wheatstacks, poplars, and cathedral façades. A composition almost identical to the Courtauld picture (private collection) is distinct in light and colour, being tinged with the warm orange tones of a setting sun.

In 1888, Monet worked on several canvases at the same time in order to prepare for a special exhibition. Theo van Gogh showed ten of the landscapes late in 1888, and the following year seventeen views of Antibes were exhibited together as Monet intended. The Mediterranean canvases confounded some observers who found in them a "poetic vagueness" and "garish originality." Gustave Geffroy, on the other hand, warmly applauded the satisfying and relaxing aspects of the landscapes, hailing Monet as "the poet and historian of the south of France." A.C.

_____

1. Joachim Pissarro, *Monet and the Mediterranean*, exh. cat., Kimbell Art Museum, Fort Worth, 1997, p. 44.

Courtauld and His American Counterparts

A Humanist Vision

Samuel Courtauld began collecting his extraordinary Impressionist and Post-Impressionist pictures at the beginning of the 1920s. His interest had been piqued by two earlier British collectors, Sir Hugh Lane and Miss Gwendoline Davies. Lane's Impressionist pictures were shown at the Tate Gallery in 1917 (fig. 14) and a selection from Davies' collection was highlighted in a 1922 exhibition of French paintings at the Burlington Fine Arts Club.

It was during this expansive decade that a dynamic group of American collectors was equally intent on assembling great art collections. What exactly do the collections of Courtauld and his American counterparts, Dr. Albert Barnes (1872–1951) and Duncan Phillips (1886–1966), reveal of their personal taste and collecting philosophies? While different artists and types of art stirred their emotions, all three collected modern French painting with passion. Regardless of their nationality, they shared a humanist vision of art, embracing the notion that works of art could elevate the human spirit. They believed that art could enrich the lives of those it touched.

Samuel Courtauld professed that works of art were meant to be loved and experienced. Analysing and understanding these emotions evoked when looking at art was paramount. He believed that "unfettered imagination, human emotion and spiritual aspiration go to the creation of all great works, and a share of the same qualities is needed for the reading of them." Courtauld espoused the timeless value of art and its civilizing influence when he wrote in *Ideals and Industry*, "Art is universal and eternal; it ties race to race, and epoch to epoch. It overleaps divisions and unites men in one all-embracing and disinterested and living pursuit."[1]

Albert Barnes expressed the similar belief: "If the creative impulse leaves its mark in a material that generates similar feelings in other people, the work of art is a human document of permanent worth. Its degree of worth is determined by the extent to which the artist has enriched, improved, [and] humanized the common experience of man in the world in which he lives."[2] This humanist approach to understanding art was further upheld by fellow collector Duncan Phillips: "Art is part of the social purpose of the world and requires appreciation and the bonds of fellowship with all who share and understand."[3]

Courtauld, Barnes, and Phillips ultimately believed in the civilizing and socially unifying forces of art which prompted their deep commitment to public education. And with remarkable largesse, all three deliberately shaped their extraordinary collections to achieve that ideal.

Fig. 14. Renoir, *Les Parapluies*, around 1881–1885, National Gallery, London. Bequeathed to the National Gallery by Sir Hugh Lane, this painting was greatly admired by Samuel Courtauld.

Art Institutions

In 1931, with the express intention that his magnificent personal collection of Impressionist and Post-Impressionist paintings be accessible to students and the public, Samuel Courtauld established the Courtauld Institute of Art. Here young teachers, museum curators and administrators could be trained to educate the public. While an advocate for studies in the history of art, he did not endorse a program of pure academic scholarship: the institute should teach more than "history alone ... [and] what we endeavour to teach there is art appreciation."[4] His own appreciation for art did not come from an academic understanding but from a heartfelt and spontaneous aesthetic reaction. He passionately believed in the democracy of art education and felt it should not be "reserved for the wealthy, the idle and the learned...."[5] Central to this philosophy was his conviction that an educated public was the key to a unified and productive society.

This same democratic principle was shared by Dr. Albert Barnes who opened his own educational facility in 1925. The Barnes Foundation, in Merion, Pennsylvania, offered to its students "something basically objective to replace the sentimentalism, the antiquarianism, sheltered under the cloak of academic prestige, which make futile the present courses in art in universities and colleges generally."[6]

But, while Barnes and Courtauld shared educational philosophies, they differed in their approach. Barnes's rigid educational method stressed an objective way of looking at art. Organized as a teaching institution with limited public access, he used his galleries as scientific laboratories, where he installed and boldly juxtaposed all types of art from different cultures, periods, and media. Thus, Renoir, Cézanne, and Matisse were interspersed amid an array of African, Islamic, Chinese, and Native American art. Students were encouraged to recognize the unifying forms in works of art and the concept of multiculturalism. Deeply suspicious of the museum world, he not only prohibited the loan of his works to exhibitions, he often refused curators access to the collection.

Based upon the same principles as Courtauld and Barnes, Duncan Phillips established the Phillips Memorial Art Gallery in 1921. Works of art were displayed in the domestic interiors of his private residence in Washington. Unlike Barnes's dogmatic and governing approach to education, his broader educational philosophy was much closer to Courtauld's. He wrote, "The Phillips Collection is based on a definite policy of supporting many methods of seeing and painting." Phillips's great desire was "to see the day when no college will be considered adequate which does not offer courses in the theory and philosophy of art in the artist's point of view."[7] His gallery was open to the public and enhanced with special exhibitions, publications, docent services, lectures, and concerts. M.K.

---

1. Quoted by House, *Impressionism for England*, p. 35.

2. Richard J. Wattenmaker and Anne Distel, *Great French Paintings from the Barnes Foundation*, New York, 1993, pp. 9–10.

3. Duncan Phillips, *A Collection in the Making*, New York, 1926, p. 5.

4. House, *Impressionism for England*, p. 29.

5. Ibid., p. 43.

6. Albert C. Barnes, *The Art in Painting*, New York, 1926, p. x.

7. Phillips, *A Collection in the Making*, pp. 6, 10.

Camille Pissarro
St. Thomas (Danish Virgin Islands) 1830-1903 Paris

[24]

CAMILLE PISSARRO
Lordship Lane Station, Dulwich 1871

oil on canvas, 44.5 x 72.5 cm
signed lower right: C. Pissarro 1871
HISTORY: Alexander Rosenberg, Paris. Lazare Weiler, Paris
(auctioned 1901). Tavernier, Paris. Pearson, Paris (auctioned in Berlin,
1927). Auctioned in Paris, 1928. Bought by Samuel Courtauld in 1936
from A. Tooth & Sons, London. Courtauld Bequest 1948.

During the Franco-Prussian War of 1870-1871, Pissarro left besieged Paris for London, settling in Norwood, a southern suburb. Seen in this painting is Lordship Lane Station at nearby Dulwich. The railway line had been completed only in 1865 to provide direct transportation to the Crystal Palace, the central structure of the Great Exhibition of 1851 which had been moved from central London to the southern suburbs in 1854, and had been drawing huge crowds. The painting thus depicts a "new" landscape: at its centre, a modern transportation link to the developing outskirts of the city. This theme was often favoured by Impressionist painters in the 1870s and 1880s,

but this appears to be the first painting by a member of the group to show a train as principal subject.

The scattered dabs of browns and greys evoke an overcast, monochromatic day. Typical of early Impressionist pictures, the subdued green tones are derived from Camille Corot's use of grey-green. The houses, trees, and roads appear flat against distant sweeping hills, a compositional device favoured by Pissarro in his paintings of Pontoise made later in the 1870s. X-radiographs and infra-red photographs show that there was originally a figure in the foreground on the slope to the right of the tracks. A.C.

{25}

CAMILLE PISSARRO
Festival at L'Hermitage around 1876

oil on canvas, 46.5 x 55.1 cm
signed lower left: Pissarro
HISTORY: Durand-Ruel, Paris; sold in 1913 to Paul Cassirer & Co.,
Berlin. Louis Ullstein, Berlin. Bought by Count Antoine Seilern
in 1941 in London. Seilern Bequest 1978
(Princes Gate Collection).

This rapidly painted composition appears only partly finished. Depicted here is a street in L'Hermitage, a suburb of
Pontoise where Pissarro lived. Although Pontoise is only
about thirty-two kilometres from Paris, the scene here is
one of a rural village, animated by the crowds around the
temporary stalls set up for a festival. We do not know what
is being celebrated; it may well be a local religious festival.

Throughout the picture, Pissarro sought to create the
most vigorous effect through both brushwork and colour.

The touch is extremely varied, but emphatic and animated throughout, registering the textures of the scene
with a bold shorthand. Detail is virtually obliterated:
the faces are simple dabs of colour, but the clothing of
the figures is closely enough defined to make clear the
mix of classes in the crowd. Such festivals were among
the few occasions where upper and lower classes would
have mingled as freely as this.

[26]

CAMILLE PISSARRO
The Quays at Rouen 1883

oil on canvas, 46.3 x 55.7 cm
signed lower left: C. Pissarro, 1883
HISTORY: Private collection, Berlin. Bought by Samuel Courtauld
in 1926 from Paul Cassirer, Berlin. Courtauld Gift 1932.

In the autumn of 1883, Pissarro visited Rouen. Fascinated by the many unusual vistas and the variety of subjects, Pissarro stayed for nearly three months in the city, painting thirteen canvases which show the boating and industrial activities along the banks of the Seine.

In this picture, a wide street gives way to boats docked along the quay. Nestled under the hills on the opposite bank are busy factories churning out steam and smoke. The silhouette of the hills is crowned by the nineteenth-century church of Notre-Dame de Bonsecours. Rouen was in fact a much bigger industrial city than this particular image suggests, and many of Pissarro's other depictions of the city pulsate with human and commercial activity (fig. 15). Here, a note of calm is introduced by the expansive foreground and the broad sweep of the hills in back. While there are many individual dabs of bright colour, Pissarro gives the painting an overall unifying monochrome tone suggestive of bright sunshine filtered through haze.

Pissarro was especially fond of painting the bustle of urban life, and returned to Rouen for lengthy periods in 1896 and 1898, making an extensive series of paintings. M.K.

Fig. 15. Pissarro, *The Boieldieu Bridge in Rouen; Wet Weather*, 1896, Art Gallery of Ontario, Toronto.

Berthe Morisot
Bourges 1841-1895 Paris

[27]

BERTHE MORISOT
Portrait of a Woman around 1872

oil on canvas, 56 x 46.1 cm
signed upper left: B. Morisot
HISTORY: Galerie Miethke, Vienna. Baron Adolf Kohner, Budapest
(by 1904; auctioned in Budapest, 1934), bought by Count Antoine
Seilern. Seilern Bequest 1978 (Princes Gate Collection).

The sitter has been identified as a Madame Heude or the artist's sister Edma. However, the other known portraits of Edma Pontillon show a face different in shape and proportion from those of the woman depicted here.

Morisot's technique combines broad fluent sweeps of paint with delicate but freely applied points of emphasis that indicate the decoration of the dress without any recourse to precise detailing. This handling reflects the example of Manet, with whom Morisot worked closely in these years, but the finesse of the touch here, especially in the white lacework around the sitter's neck, is fully characteristic of Morisot. The colour scheme is quite subdued, based around soft greys, beiges, browns, and pinks, set against the sharp purple accent of the flowers on the sitter's bosom and the intense blue brooch at her neck, which is picked up in the soft light blues in the white lace below it. At this point in the centre of the picture, the black choker around her neck contrasts sharply with the white lace. It was by these subtle pictorial devices that Morisot organized her composition.

Alfred Sisley
Paris 1839–1899 Moret-sur-Loing

[28]

ALFRED SISLEY
Snow at Louveciennes 1874
oil on canvas, 46.3 x 55.8 cm
signed lower right: Sisley
HISTORY: Bought by Samuel Courtauld in 1926 from the
Independent Gallery, London. Courtauld Gift 1932.

[29]

ALFRED SISLEY

Boats on the Seine around 1877

oil on canvas, 37.2 x 44.3 cm
signed lower right: Sisley
HISTORY: Perhaps Richard Samson, Hamburg.
Bought by Samuel Courtauld in 1947 from the Matthiesen Gallery,
London. Courtauld Bequest 1948.

By 1877, Sisley's brushwork had become more broken and energetic. The small scale of this canvas heightens the effect of sketchiness and immediacy, clearly conveying the feeling of a windy day with its rapidly changing cloud formations. All of the Impressionists painted small, gestural oil sketches along with larger, more finished canvases intended for the market.

This view of the Seine at Billancourt, at the southwest edge of Paris, depicts the somewhat subdued economic activities of the suburbs. A single barge is being unloaded as a passenger ferry passes nearby. Otherwise, little else is happening. Neither city nor country, the site possesses pictorial elements of both. A.C.

Pierre-Auguste Renoir
Limoges 1841-1919 Cagnes-sur-Mer

[30]

PIERRE–AUGUSTE RENOIR

La Loge 1874

oil on canvas, 80 x 63.5 cm
signed lower left: A. Renoir. 74.
HISTORY: Exhibited at the first Impressionist exhibition, Paris, 1874,
and later the same year in London; sold in 1875 to the dealer Martin,
Paris. M. Fleurnois, Paris; sold in 1899 to Durand-Ruel, Paris;
bought by Samuel Courtauld in 1925 through Percy Moore Turner.
Courtauld Bequest 1948.

La Loge was one of seven works which Renoir showed at the first Impressionist exhibition held in 1874, an event which gave birth to the term "Impressionism" because of the title of Monet's painting, *Impression, soleil levant* (*Impression, Rising Sun*, Musée Marmottan, Paris). *La Loge* was very well received and can be regarded as the hit of the show, both the technique and the subject appealing even to traditional critics. Although the published catalogue of the Impressionist exhibition gives Renoir's title as "La Loge," at one point it seems to have been called "Avant-scène" (Before the Stage) since this is how most reviewers referred to it. Theatrical subjects were immensely popular with the Impressionists in the 1870s, especially with Degas and Mary Cassatt.

In *La Loge*, the woman has put down her opera glasses in order to display herself and her costume. Perhaps she has completed her own viewing of the audience, or of a particular individual, and now allows herself to be seen unobstructed. Or the opera glasses may simply be a prop.

Her direct stare heightens the sense of presentation. Partly shadowed, her male companion studies an upper balcony.

We sometimes assume that these gazes, exchanged glances, and binocular searches necessarily occur between members of the opposite sex and are thus infused with erotic, even voyeuristic, intentions. While this is assuredly often the case, Renoir softens his picture with ambiguity. Is the man scanning the "cheap seats" for available women? Is the woman herself a garishly dressed and promiscuous "cocotte," or an elegant lady fashionably attired. Contemporary viewers were themselves unsure.

The soft, shimmering brushstrokes direct attention to the play of light on the translucent fabrics of the dress. Renoir's theatregoer would have commanded the attention of both male and female viewers, whether as an object of beauty, fashion, sexuality, rivalry, or curiosity. His painting is richly ambiguous in other ways. Although ostensibly a glimpse of modern life in Paris as befits a

genre picture, the work has many qualities of a portrait. The woman's face is more highly finished than the rest of the canvas, and her figure fills much of the painting's surface. The point of view is highly contrived, as though the viewer were suspended in the theatre just beyond the loge.

In 1874, Renoir exhibited two other paintings which depict female types, *The Dancer* (fig. 16) and *Parisienne* (fig. 17). This trio has a programmatic intent which predicts Tissot's series of 1885, *The Parisian Woman* (La femme à Paris).

After the Impressionist exhibition, *La Loge* was exhibited in London in November of 1874, making it one of the first paintings by Renoir to be seen in Britain. It was one of Samuel Courtauld's most cherished pictures, and he wrote a short poem about it around 1939. Courtauld described the power which Renoir had

of conveying quietly but very firmly the solid structure beneath a tender and evanescent surface. No other impressionist did this, yet none ever rendered the subtle charm of surfaces, the colour of atmosphere, or the beauties of texture, with so sensitive and rich a brush as he.[1]

A.C.

---

1. Samuel Courtauld, *Pictures into Verse*, privately printed around 1939, p. 62, note 11. Quoted by Dennis Farr in *Impressionist and Post-Impressionist Masterpieces: The Courtauld Collection*, exh. cat. Cleveland Museum of Art, et al., 1987, p. 10.

Fig. 16. Renoir, *The Dancer*, 1874, National Gallery of Art, Washington.

Fig. 17. Renoir, *Parisienne*, 1874, National Museums and Galleries of Wales, Cardiff.

[31]

PIERRE–AUGUSTE RENOIR

The Outskirts of Pont-Aven around 1892

oil on canvas, 54.5 x 65 cm
signed lower left: Renoir

HISTORY: Bought by Count Antoine Seilern in 1942 from
Alex. Reid & Lefèvre, London. Seilern Bequest 1978
(Princes Gate Collection).

[32]

PIERRE–AUGUSTE RENOIR
Woman at Her Toilet around 1918

oil on canvas, 50.5 x 56.5 cm
signed lower left: Renoir
HISTORY: Bought by Samuel Courtauld in 1922 from
Percy Moore Turner. Courtauld Gift 1932.

Paul Cézanne
Aix-en-Provence 1839-1906 Aix-en-Provence

[33]

PAUL CÉZANNE

Tall Trees at the Jas de Bouffan 1885-1887

oil on canvas, 65 x 81 cm

HISTORY: Ambroise Vollard, Paris. Paul Rosenberg, Paris, 1922; sold in 1924 to Samuel Courtauld. Courtauld Bequest 1948.

In 1859, Cézanne's father bought an estate just outside Aix-en-Provence called the Jas de Bouffan. Cézanne frequently painted the grounds and worked in a studio in the house until 1899 when he sold the property.

On this lightly worked canvas, individual brushstrokes can be clearly seen as separately applied marks of paint. Although placed in parallel patterns throughout the work, the strokes never form purely geometrical patterns, but vary subtly according to what is represented, giving the picture an overall rhythm. The electricity of the technique seems perfectly suited to the subject of rustling foliage lit from behind by a bright sky. The date and technique are very close to the *Interior of a Forest* in the Art Gallery of Ontario (fig. 18).

Subtle devices anchor the composition of *Tall Trees at the Jas de Bouffan*. The straight line of the garden wall creates a base for the tree trunks which are boldly outlined in dark paint. In the foliage, lighter tones of green are scattered amidst much darker shades. Finally, the warm orange tones of buildings or fields frame the composition at left and right. A.C.

Fig. 18. Cézanne, *Interior of a Forest*, around 1885, Art Gallery of Ontario, Toronto.

[34]

PAUL CÉZANNE
L'Étang des Sœurs, Osny 1877

oil on canvas, 60 x 73.5 cm
HISTORY: Camille Pissarro, Paris. Alphonse Kann,
Saint-German-en-Laye. Hugo von Reininghaus, Vienna.
Galerie Barbazanges, Paris. Alex. Reid, Glasgow.
Bought by Samuel Courtauld in 1923 from Thos. Agnew & Sons,
London. Courtauld Gift 1932.

In this picture, the paint has largely been applied with a palette knife. This is especially noticeable in the long diagonal lines which make up the foliage, as well as in the sweeping horizontal bands of the foreground. The knife often leaves a straight ridge of oil paint on one side of the stroke. This technique calls attention to the physical substance of paint in a manner very similar to the late landscapes of Gustave Courbet (1819-1877), who had just died when this work was made.

The painting is among the first of Cézanne's compositions constructed of blocks of colour arranged in parallel rows. Lawrence Gowing wrote:

It was in 1877 that colour differentiation took its place as a chief medium of definition in Cézanne's art, and no picture has a more crucial place in his development.[1]

Although Pissarro and the Impressionists sometimes painted dense wooded scenes similar to this landscape, they usually included figures, paths, or other signs of human activity. Even at this early stage, Cézanne's view of landscape focuses more directly on nature; the absence of civilizing forces in *L'Étang des Sœurs, Osny* creates a lonely scene. A.C.

1. Lawrence Gowing, *Cézanne: The Late Work*, exh. cat., Museum of Modern Art, New York, 1977, pp. 5-6.

[35]

PAUL CÉZANNE

A Shed around 1880

pencil and watercolour on paper, 31.4 x 47.5 cm
HISTORY: Bought by Samuel Courtauld from Paul Rosenberg, Paris.
Courtauld Gift 1932.

[36]

PAUL CÉZANNE

Study of a Tree 1885–1887

pencil on paper, 31.5 x 47.8 cm
HISTORY: Found in 1981 unregistered in the Courtauld Gallery.

PAUL CÉZANNE

Mont Sainte-Victoire around 1887

oil on canvas, 66.8 x 92.3 cm
signed lower right: P. Cézanne
HISTORY: Given in 1896 to Joachim Gasquet, Aix-en-Provence;
sold by Gasquet in 1908 to Galerie Bernheim-Jeune, Paris; sold in
1925 to Samuel Courtauld. Courtauld Gift 1934.

Cézanne had been familiar with Mont Sainte-Victoire since childhood, and in the 1880s executed a series of images of the peak which defined his mature style. Together with a second series made between 1901 and 1906, these views are among the most celebrated in art history. Houses and fields, rendered in green and ochre, fill the Arc River valley, as the mountain rises in blue tones. In the right distance is a railway viaduct. A pine tree at the left extends its branches over the panorama, to be met by the limbs of another tree.

One of the most remarkable elements of the painting is the pattern of foliage which follows the silhouette of the mountain quite precisely. Combined with the vertical trunk at the left, the trees frame the view of the peak. Here, the perspective is deliberately confused, as background and foreground seem to mix and overlap. The rich, energetic brushwork contributes to this sensation, especially in the electric effect of the branches and foliage silhouetted against the sky. Indeed, the pine trees threaten to become the dominant element in the painting, absorbing the mountain into their twisting forms.

At almost the same time, Cézanne painted a very similar view, but in a rather different technique and with an altogether different result (fig. 19). This was acquired by Duncan Phillips in 1925, precisely the same year Samuel Courtauld bought his painting of Mont Sainte-Victoire. Phillips was the other great collector of Impressionist and Post-Impressionist pictures active in the 1920s and their collections make interesting comparison. In the Phillips painting, the valley and mountain occupy a much larger part of the composition, while the wall and viaduct, which recede into the landscape in the Courtauld picture, form a dominant design. The brushwork in the Phillips painting is spare, with much of the canvas priming showing through. However coincidentally, the difference between the two paintings reflect the difference in taste between the two collectors, with Courtauld being more conservative and Phillips much more interested in art of the twentieth century.

In 1895, some eight years after the Courtauld painting had been finished, Cézanne submitted it to a small exhibition in Aix-en-Provence. A young poet, Joachim Gasquet, praised the work enthusiastically. Cézanne immediately signed the painting and gave it to the surprised Gasquet. Gasquet, who became a friend and biographer of Cézanne, provided a later, somewhat embellished account of the making of the painting:

> He had planted his easel in the shade of a clump of pines. He was at his brother-in-law's, where he had been working for two months on one canvas in the morning, another in the afternoon. The work was "going well." The work was nearing its end and he was in a happy frame of mind.
>
> The canvas was gradually becoming denser and more balanced. The preconceived image, well thought out and linear in its logic, which he must have sketched in with rapid charcoal strokes, in his usual manner, already emerged from the coloured patches that everywhere surrounded it. The landscape seemed to shimmer, for Cézanne had slowly worked around each object, sampling, as it were, each colour; day by day, imperceptibly, he had brought together all these values with an unerring sense of harmony, in a relationship at once subdued and glowing.[1]

A.C.

_____

1. Joachim Gasquet, *Cézanne*, Paris, 1921, p. 79.

Fig. 19. Cézanne, *Mont Saint-Victoire*, 1886–1887, The Phillips Collection, Washington.

[38]
PAUL CÉZANNE
Mont Sainte-Victoire 1885–1887
pencil and watercolour on paper, 32.8 x 50.5 cm
HISTORY: Sold by the artist's son in 1907 to Bernheim-Jeune, Paris.
G. F. Reber, Lausanne. Bought by Samuel Courtauld in 1924 from
the Independent Gallery, London. Courtauld Gift 1932.

This view of Mont Sainte-Victoire belongs to the same period as the painting of subject (cat. 37), but appears to have been made in the valley itself, much closer to the mountain. The point of view relates closely to a painting in the Barnes Foundation.

The drawing was shown in the first Cézanne exhibition ever held in North America, arranged in March 1911 by Alfred Stieglitz in his Photo-Secession Gallery, New York. The reviewer for the *New York Times* wrote of the picture:

One fine little landscape, a mountain that might be Fuji-yama, but appears in the catalogue as "Mount Victoire" rising very solid, very dignified, and serene, is modeled with a few forcible strokes of pale greenish grayish neutral color. There is so little to say about the picture, and it is so potent to stir the imagination of the lover of nature, that one is tempted to leave the rest of the exhibition alone and go an inch or two into the cause and effect of this kind of art.[1]

For Lawrence Gowing, Cézanne's abstract vision of landscape was best seen in this drawing rather than in the paintings of Mont Sainte-Victoire. "Diluted tones are placed in a wide-spaced series—yellow-green, emerald, and blue-gray. It is an emergent logic in the order, rather than anything one can imagine observing on the spot, that reconstructs the mass of the trees and links it with the mountain behind."[2] A.C.

---

1. John Rewald, in *Paul Cézanne: The Watercolours*, Boston, 1983, no. 279, identifies the work as number 8 in the Photo-Secession exhibition, and quotes the review from the *New York Times* of 13 March 1911 (perhaps by Elizabeth Luther Clay).
2. Gowing, *Cézanne*, p. 58.

[39]

PAUL CÉZANNE

Pot of Flowers and Fruit 1888–1890

oil on canvas, 46 x 56.2 cm

HISTORY: Bought by Samuel Courtauld in 1928 from Alex.
Reid & Lefèvre, London. Courtauld Bequest 1948.

[40]

PAUL CÉZANNE

The Cardplayers 1893–1896

oil on canvas, 60 x 73 cm

HISTORY: Ambroise Vollard, Paris (exhibited at Paul Cassirer,
Berlin, 1904). Dr. Julius Elias, Berlin. J. B. Stang, Oslo.
Bought by Samuel Courtauld in 1929 from Alfred Gold, Berlin.
Courtauld Gift 1932.

Beginning in 1890, Cézanne painted the local people who worked on his estate outside Aix-en-Provence, or who lived nearby. Besides single figures (cat. 41), the artist made a series of paintings of men playing cards. These seem to have been based on drawings of individual figures, rather than on groups posed in the studio. Roger Fry, who was Cézanne's greatest advocate in Britain, described the paintings of cardplayers:

It is hard to think of any design since those of the great Italian Primitives — one or two of Rembrandt's later pieces might perhaps be cited — which gives us so extraordinary a sense of monumental gravity and resistance — of something that has found its centre and can never be moved.[1]

At first Cézanne's paintings contained several figures. The painting in the Barnes Foundation of 1890-1891 shows three men playing cards with a young girl and a man looking on. Somewhat later, Cézanne painted the work reproduced here which contains only two figures (there are two other versions of this composition, one larger, one smaller).

The mood of the Courtauld painting is dark and still. With few distracting details, the two men stare with intense concentration at their cards. The tablecloth and legs are painted in uniform brown tones, while the background is also a dark mesh of blues and blacks. Intense in shadow and monumental in effect, Cézanne has distilled his original concept to its essential elements.

This subject calls attention to Cézanne's abiding love for his native region, which found expression not only in landscapes of Mont Sainte-Victoire, but in the local inhabitants who were so deeply connected to the land. A.C.

―――――――

1. Roger Fry, *Cézanne: A Study of His Development*, London, 1927, p. 72.

[41]
PAUL CÉZANNE
Man with a Pipe around 1896
oil on canvas, 73 x 60 cm
HISTORY: Paul Gallimard, Paris. Louis Hodebert, Paris.
Galerie E. Bignou, Paris. Bought by Samuel Courtauld in 1927 from
Alex. Reid & Lefèvre, London. Courtauld Gift 1932.

The man depicted here was also the model for the figure on the left in *The Cardplayers* (cat. 40) and for several other paintings. This most patient of Cézanne's models was apparently Alexandre Paulin, a gardener at Jas de Bouffan, the artist's estate. Cézanne seems to have found a sympathetic personality in this worker, for there is a serene yet attentive gaze in the face depicted here. Louis Vauxcelles in 1905 described Cézanne's models as "shifty, obstinate peasants," but Lionello Venturi found Paulin to be "one of those popular personalities, full of energy and power that inspired sympathy and admiration in Cézanne."

Paint has been applied in diagonal patterns which are remarkably consistent throughout the painting, and seem to derive the incisive angle of the man's pipe. The overall sombre tone of the painting accents the warm tones of the face and a scattering of lighter highlights in the hat and jacket. A.C.

[42]

PAUL CÉZANNE
Lac d'Annecy 1896

oil on canvas, 65 x 81 cm
HISTORY: Sold by the artist in 1897 to Ambroise Vollard, Paris, and
sold shortly thereafter to Cornelis Hoogendijk, Amsterdam.
Paul Rosenberg, Paris. Marcel Kapferer, Paris, sold in 1925 to
Galerie Bernheim-Jeune, Paris; sold in 1926 to the
Independent Gallery, London, which sold it the same year to
Samuel Courtauld. Courtauld Gift 1932.

Lac d'Annecy is one of Cézanne's most insistently abstract and geometric compositions. The repetition of parallel blocks of paint leading from the lake to the mountains, the sky, and finally to the branches of the tree is rigorous and prismatic in effect.

At the urging of his family, Cézanne spent July and August of 1896 on Lake Annecy, a bustling summer resort. Only a handful of watercolours and this single painting resulted from the stay. Cézanne may have had difficulties finding appropriate motifs because the rugged terrain was not only unfamiliar to him but also conventionally picturesque. He wrote:

The height of the surrounding mountains is quite considerable, the lake which is narrowed here by two tongues of land seems to lend itself to the linear exercises of young English misses. It is still nature, of course, but a bit like we've learned to see it in the travel sketchbooks of young ladies.[1]

In searching for the unconventional, Cézanne created a stifling, almost sinister landscape. The tree reaches into the landscape, crystallizing its forms; the lake is transformed into "a kind of bottomless Styx." The emotional intensity of the picture may be the result of the artist's state of mind; he complained, "Life for me is beginning to be of sepulchre monotony…. To relieve my boredom, I paint; it is not much fun." A.C.

1. Letter from Cézanne to Joachim Gasquet; *Cézanne Correspondance*, ed. J. Rewald, Paris, 1978, p. 253.

84

[43]

PAUL CÉZANNE

Apples, Bottle and Chairback around 1900–1906

pencil and gouache on paper, 45.8 x 60.4 cm
HISTORY: Paul, the artist's son. Justin K. Thannhauser, Berlin.
Bought by Samuel Courtauld in 1937 from Wildenstein & Co.
Courtauld Bequest 1948.

Towards the end of his life, Cézanne made a series of still lifes in watercolour which are remarkable for their large scale and sense of freedom and movement. The curvaceous forms and brilliant colours give the work a joyous, light-hearted mood. Lawrence Gowing wrote in 1973:

In this still-life from the Courtauld Institute the arcs of colour, convex and concave in turn, interlocking with the whiteness of the paper, echo backwards up the pile of fruit to reach their summit in the chair-back. There is a ceremonious elaboration about them, yet innumerable hours in the Louvre spent on the study of how the spring and recoil of rhythm made volume manifest must have contributed to such an image.[1]

A.C.

_____

1. Gowing, *Watercolour and Pencil Drawings by Cézanne*, exh. cat., Newcastle, 1973, no. 98.

[44]
PAUL CÉZANNE
The Turning Road around 1904
oil on canvas, 73 x 92 cm
HISTORY: Ambroise Vollard, Paris. Sir Kenneth Clark,
sold in 1941 to Count Antoine Seilern. Seilern Bequest 1978
(Princes Gate Collection).

Although it is one of his largest landscapes, *The Turning Road* is a very lightly worked picture, with large areas of the light-toned primed canvas left unpainted. In the second half of his career, Cézanne abandoned many canvases at a similarly early stage of their execution, when in conventional terms they were clearly unfinished. However, he considered even some of his most highly worked paintings to be in some sense unsatisfactory and incomplete, while there are unfinished areas in many paintings that he seems to have felt to be fully resolved.

The lack of finish in Cézanne's late paintings has been a powerful inspiration for many artists in the twentieth century in their search for an expressive personal style that rejected academic rules. In contrast to the loose finish of the picture, the subject is conventional, with a village in the distance dominated by a church spire, and the composition framed on the left by a pair of trees. The site represented has not been identified, but it has been suggested that it is a scene near Cézanne's last studio at Chemin des Lauves on the northern edge of Aix-en-Provence. However, it may well be a scene from northern France; Cézanne was painting near Fontainebleau in 1904. The flatness of the landscape depicted and the comparatively muted colour suggest a northern site.

Collecting Strategies

The Discerning Eye

Courtauld purposefully did not amass an enormous and diverse collection. Instead, he collected in a more prescribed manner what he considered to be the "best" Impressionist and Post-Impressionist pictures, and bought with a discerning eye. The purchase of Renoir's spectacular *La Loge* (cat. 30), reflects his interest in both the aesthetic appeal and historical importance of a painting. Initially attracted to the breathtaking beauty of *La Loge*, Courtauld was equally drawn to its significance as one of the paintings shown in the first Impressionist exhibition of 1874. Manet's late masterpiece *A Bar at the Folies-Bergère* (cat. 14) and Degas' *Ballet Scene* (cat. 16) were also acquired for their artistic merits. Similarly, Duncan Phillips purchased Renoir's *Luncheon of the Boating Party* (fig. 20) for its exceptional aesthetic qualities but also to attract attention to his collection.

Courtauld was not interested in forming encyclopedic holdings of particular artists. Compare his purchase of eight paintings by Renoir to the 180 owned by the formidable Dr. Barnes. For Barnes, the opportunity to study in depth and breadth one of his favourite artist's was essential. There were pictures of great beauty and importance, as well as those which were minor and insignificant. Instead of amassing an uneven group of paintings for study, Courtauld acquired selectively, a process he described as "subjective — and sentimental — romantic, and ... I love every kind of beauty."[1]

While Courtauld's collection represents outstanding examples of works by such Post-Impressionist painters as Cézanne, Gauguin, Van Gogh, Seurat, and Toulouse-Lautrec, he did not collect the more avant-garde schools. Nor did the art of other cultures influence his collecting practices. With a single-minded devotion to the French artists he championed, he saw no reason to collect in other areas. Anthony Blunt, former director of the Courtauld Institute, commented that "he was not remotely interested in knowing what he ought to buy, and the concept of what was fashionable, or what was admired by the best authorities, was of no significance to him."[2]

Courtauld did not, for the most part, consult dealers or experts. After finding a picture in London, Paris, or New York, Courtauld would first take it home to see if it properly suited his aesthetic criteria and domestic environment. "Being one of those people who live chiefly by the eye," he said, "I have found my most lasting aesthetic pleasure in looking at pictures...."[3] And once having found that pleasure met in a particular work of art, he would then, naturally, acquire it. M.K.

---

1. House, *Impressionism for England*, p. 29.

2. Blunt in Cooper, *The Courtauld Collection*, p. 4.

3. Cooper, *The Courtauld Collection*, p. 8.

Fig. 20. Renoir, *Luncheon of the Boating Party*, 1881, The Phillips Collection, Washington.

Selective Tastes

Samuel Courtauld's collection generally reflected the conventional wisdoms and canons of the 1920s. The best Impressionist paintings in the collection are the figural works by Manet, Degas, and Renoir. Landscapes seem to have been less important to Courtauld, with the major exception of the mature works by Cézanne which represent a comprehensive survey of the highest quality.

Guided by a purely personal sense of aesthetic quality, and often disdainful of historical principles, nonetheless, Courtauld's collecting comprised great subtlety and a sense of historical precision. His selection of subjects reveals a consistent vision between his personal collection and the works he bought for the Tate Gallery. The works by Manet, for example, both depict waitresses at theatrical cafés (fig. 6 and cat. 14). Two paintings by Renoir show young women attending the theatre (cat. 30), while several theatrical subjects occur in Courtauld's works by Degas. He collected three artists with a special passion: Renoir, Cézanne, and Seurat. Six paintings by Renoir were in the personal collection, and two more were bought for the Tate Gallery. The range of pictures by Cézanne is comprehensive, carefully covering almost all periods and most genres; the artist's early figural paintings are absent, but they were not all well known in the 1920s. The group of paintings by Seurat, including *Une baignade* in the National Gallery, is equally impressive.

There are well-known limitations to Courtauld's collecting, and he is often faulted for not pursuing Modernism and the work of living artists. In general, the collection was confined to the mainstreams of Impressionism and Post-Impressionism, avoiding the Realist movement and the Barbizon school (Daumier and Boudin being the exceptions), and, with a single exception, the paintings of Picasso, Braque, and Matisse. His approach to the work of Monet is also curious. In 1923, he bought the still life and the Antibes landscape, and, in May 1924, *Autumn Effect* (cats. 21, 22, 23). While these three works are striking examples, they are not at all typical works and must have seemed bizarre at the time, given the almost studious selectivity applied to other painters. A.C.

Paul Gauguin
Paris 1848-1903 Atuona (Marquesas Islands)

[45]

PAUL GAUGUIN
The Haystacks 1889
oil on canvas, 92 x 73.3 cm
signed lower right: P. Gauguin '89
HISTORY: Ambroise Vollard, Paris. Dr. Frizeau, Bordeaux.
Bought by Samuel Courtauld in 1923 from Jos. Hessel, Paris.
Courtauld Gift 1932.

Before Gauguin left France in 1891 to paint the exotic culture of Tahiti, he discovered a retreat from Paris in the small rural community of Pont-Aven in Brittany. Since the early nineteenth century, artists such as Boudin, Daubigny, Monet, and Whistler had painted there, encouraging a thriving art colony by the late 1880s. Although the annual invasion of artists did not impress Gauguin, he established friendships with a group of young painters that included Émile Bernard, Paul Sérusier, and Jacob Meyer de Haan. Together they decided to live simply and observe the native aspects of local Breton life which they considered more suitable for painting than subjects offered by the urban sophistication of Paris which the Impressionists had favoured.

The Haystacks is the second painting of Breton peasants at work which Gauguin made during the summer of 1889 at Pont-Aven. This decorative picture, with its anti-naturalistic climbing perspective, demonstrates Gauguin's use of a stylistic device known as Cloisonism (so named because of its resemblance to heavily outlined cloisonné enamel) which he developed with Émile Bernard in 1888. In this painting, the composition is built with flat areas of bold and simplified colour patterns demarcated by dark contours. The head, horns, and backs of the oxen in the foreground seem to mimic the form of the haystack which thus takes on an almost anthropomorphic quality. *The Haystacks* resonates with the advice Gauguin gave in 1888:

Do not copy nature too closely. Art is an abstraction; derive it from nature while dreaming in front of it and think more of the creation which will result.

M.P.T.

[46]

PAUL GAUGUIN
Two Studies of the Head of a Bearded Man in Profile
around 1892

red chalk on paper (with some rubbing, and strokes of red
and blue watercolour), 27.3 x 17.8 cm
HISTORY: Found in 1981 unregistered in the Courtauld Gallery.

Fig. 21. Gauguin, *Male and Female Figures*, watercolour on paper (verso of the drawing).

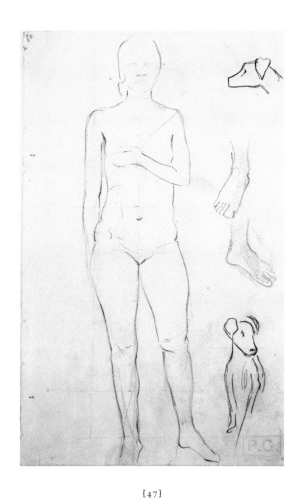

[47]

PAUL GAUGUIN

Sheet of Studies around 1892

pencil on paper, 27.3 x 17.8 cm

HISTORY: Found in 1981 unregistered in the Courtauld Gallery.

Fig. 22. Gauguin, *Man Seen from Behind*, pencil on paper (verso of the drawing).

[48]

VINCENT VAN GOGH

A Tile Factory 1888

pencil, pen and ink, on paper, 25.6 x 34.8 cm
HISTORY: J. van Gogh-Bogner, the artist's sister-in-law, Amsterdam;
her son V. W. van Gogh, Laren. Leicester Galleries, London, 1923,
sold to Samuel Courtauld in 1926. Courtauld Bequest 1948.

In March 1888, Van Gogh was living in Arles and made a large number of drawings of the surrounding country-side. After the basic composition of this drawing was indicated in pencil, Van Gogh used varying thicknesses of reed pen with an iron-gall ink to work up the composition. The reed pen responds well to different pressure while the iron-gall ink also penetrates the paper considerably. This traditional technique is a deliberate emulation of Rembrandt's drawings.

Organized in long horizontal bands, the composition of the drawing is also derived from Rembrandt and other seventeenth-century Dutch landscapists. Each layer is drawn with a distinct set of marks. Starting at the lower edge, heavy parallel lines indicate long grasses; this is followed by a series of dots, radiating diagonals, then short blunt strokes leading to the fine verticals of the fence. The regimented intensity of this scheme lays a solid foundation for the precisely detailed features of the factory building and the rather more flamboyant and energetic shape of the blossoming tree at right. A.C.

VINCENT VAN GOGH

The Crau at Arles: Peach Trees in Flower 1889

oil on canvas, 65 x 81 cm

HISTORY: Bernheim-Jeune, Paris. Bought by Samuel Courtauld in
1927 from the Independent Gallery, London. Courtauld Gift 1932.

In March of 1889, Vincent van Gogh wrote to the artist Paul Signac:

I have just come back from two studies of orchards. Here is a crude sketch of them—the big one is a poor landscape with little cottages, blue skyline of the Alpille foothills, sky white and blue. The foreground, patches of land surrounded by cane hedges, where small peach trees are in bloom—everything is small there, the gardens, the fields, the orchards and the trees, even the mountains, as in certain Japanese landscapes, which is the reason why the subject attracted me.[1]

This evidently is the painting which depicts spring blossoms in the Crau, a wide plain outside Arles. Besides the Japanese influence Van Gogh mentions, the painting also shows the influence of Impressionist colour, Pointillist brushwork, as well as compositions employed by seventeenth-century Dutch landscape painters.

Painted almost precisely a year after *A Tile Factory* (cat. 48) was made, this painting shares with that drawing a similar banded composition. Each horizontal layer stretches across a large part of the picture and possesses a characteristic brush pattern and set of colours. Van Gogh's ability to suggest a variety of textures is remarkable, seen here in the stony road with thorny grasses by its side, as well as in the soft forms of the peach blossoms. While much of the brushwork is related to Impressionism, the dazzling short strokes in the sky are startling in their intensity.

The theme of well-worked agricultural fields had been a major concern of the artist since his early years in Holland. The wide panorama was inspired by the landscapes of seventeenth-century Dutch painters Jacob van Ruisdael and especially Philips Koninck, both of whom Van Gogh mentioned frequently in his correspondence. Koninck's sweeping vistas are often ringed by distant hills brightly lit in the manner seen here. A.C.

1. *The Complete Letters of Vincent van Gogh*, vol. 3, London, 1958, pp. 149-151.

Georges Seurat
Paris 1859-1891 Paris

[50]

GEORGES SEURAT

Study for "Chahut" around 1889

oil on wood, 21.8 x 15.8 cm

HISTORY: Mme Seurat, the artist's mother, Paris. Félix Fénéon, Paris.
Bought by Samuel Courtauld in 1929 from Ambroise Vollard, Paris.
Courtauld Bequest 1948.

One of the more risqué forms of music-hall entertainment in Paris at the turn of the century was a dance called the *chahut* or the *quadrille naturaliste*. In the Montmartre cabarets frequented by artists such as Toulouse-Lautrec, Degas, as well as Seurat, prostitutes and professional dancers would perform the provocative — almost pornographic — *chahut* by kicking their legs to expose their underwear, or lack thereof, to prospective clients. Georges Seurat chose to paint the subject on this small panel after making a drawing of a performance which he witnessed at a *café-concert* called Le Divan Japonais.

The *chahut* was a perfect vehicle for the artist to explore the expressive value of colour and line as articulated in the theories of Charles Blanc and Charles Henry. Like them, Seurat believed that colours and lines could be linked to feelings and emotions. In *Study for "Chahut,"* the warm colours and the diagonal lines moving upwards to the left were meant to contribute to a "dynamogenic" effect of happiness or joy. Seurat later worked the subject into another preparatory study (Albright-Knox Art Gallery, Buffalo) before completing a larger, more finished painting (fig. 23). This final version of *Chahut* excited a great deal of controversy at the 1890 Salon des Indépendants, eclipsing *Young Woman Powdering Herself* (cat. 53) which was also exhibited on the same occasion.

Seurat's interest in applying scientific principles to painting is also witnessed in his invention of the technique called "pointillism." This device, adopted by artists associated with Neo-Impressionism such as Paul Signac, Henri Edmond Cross, and Charles Angrand, characterizes *Study for "Chahut"* as well as *Young Woman Powdering Herself* where dots of complementary colours are juxtaposed to create optical effects. Seurat even painted dots along the edges of his picture, creating a border on three sides to harmonize with and emphasize the picture surface. M.P.T.

Fig. 23. Seurat, *Chahut*, 1890, oil on canvas, Kröller-Müller Museum, Otterlo.

[51]

GEORGES SEURAT

Nude around 1881–1882

pencil and Conté crayon on paper, 63.2 x 48.2 cm
HISTORY: Inscribed by Félix Fénéon on the back. Private collection
(first exhibited at Galerie Bernheim-Jeune, Paris, in 1920 and 1926).
Bought by Samuel Courtauld in 1928 from the Independent Gallery,
London. Courtauld Bequest 1948.

When the nineteen-year-old Georges Seurat entered the drawing class taught by Henri Lehmann at the École des Beaux-Arts in 1878, he already possessed considerable technical skill. There he made copies after Raphael, Poussin, and his idol Ingres. But it was the study of antique sculpture which constituted the core of his training at the school. Most of Seurat's youthful drawings are highly finished and idealized renditions of classical Greek sculpture. These informed the way he treated the full-length nudes studied from life at the school and later in his own studio.

This drawing is typical of Seurat's mature style from the early 1880s which featured velvety black strokes of Conté crayon applied to a pale cream laid paper. Although the pose of the model is conventional, the drawing may have been made by lamplight, a departure from academic practice. The dark tones of the background against the light flesh of the woman create an effect of "irradiation" which can be found in Seurat's most accomplished drawings. He may have wished the dense blacks to evoke a look analogous to the Symbolist-inspired lithographic prints made by the popular artist Henri Fantin-Latour. M.P.T.

GEORGES SEURAT

Man Painting His Boat around 1883

oil on wood, 15.9 x 25 cm

HISTORY: recorded in the artist's posthumous inventory, 1891.
Bought by Samuel Courtauld in 1928 from the Independent Gallery,
London. Courtauld Bequest 1948
(on loan to R. A. Butler until 1983).

GEORGES SEURAT

Young Woman Powdering Herself around 1888-1890

oil on canvas, 95.5 x 79.5 cm
signed lower right: Seurat
HISTORY: Madeleine Knobloch, the artist's lover, Paris, 1891.
Félix Fénéon, Paris. Dikran Khan Kélékian, Paris (auctioned in
New York, 1923). Eugene Liston, New York. Percy Moore Turner,
London. John Quinn, New York. Paul Rosenberg, Paris.
Bought by Samuel Courtauld in 1926 from the French Gallery
(Wallis & Son), London. Courtauld Gift 1932.

Although Seurat's *Young Woman Powdering Herself* is recognized as one of the artist's masterpieces, critics took little notice of it when it was first exhibited at the 1890 Salon des Indépendants. The other figural painting which Seurat submitted, *Chahut* (fig. 23), garnered nearly all the attention. After 1887, the outdoor naturalism of Seurat's early landscapes had slowly given way to figural paintings as the artist became increasingly interested in interior scenes representative of modern life.

The model for this picture was Seurat's mistress, Madeleine Knobloch, who had just given birth to their son. An intensely private man, Seurat did not mention his companion to family and friends, who remained unaware of her until after his death from infectious diphtheria. *Young Woman Powdering Herself* is the only painting drawn from Seurat's personal life, although viewers in 1890, even close friends, would have been unaware of this intimacy.

A woman at her toilette had been a favourite subject for artists in the seventeenth and eighteenth centuries, and was taken up occasionally by nineteenth-century painters. Contrasting nature and artifice, Seurat depicts his mistress employing cosmetics in the process of turning her natural self into something artificial. While some details are closely observed, the figure seems grand and massive especially next to her impractical little table. This image suggests criticism of the stiff, unnatural trappings of modern society in Paris.

Throughout the composition, Seurat sets off rounded forms (the woman, the table legs, the powder puff) with sharp angles (the mirror, the picture on the wall, the woman's bodice, the bend of her right arm). The flat, confined space allows Seurat to contrast, and perhaps mock, the robust figure of Madeleine with the spindly domestic objects.

Seurat created his painting with a network of small brushstrokes consisting of complementary colours, as is typical of Pointillism. More dots of paint were applied over the basic pattern so that the forms seem solid and luminous when viewed from a distance. Warm and cool colours are interwoven to create a shimmering effect. Seurat had developed this highly systematic and supposedly scientific technique in response to the freer and more intuitive approach to painting used by the Impressionists. He also sought to evoke permanence and solidity: "I want to make modern people, in their essential traits, move about as they do in frescoes and place them on canvases organized by harmonies of colours." M.K.

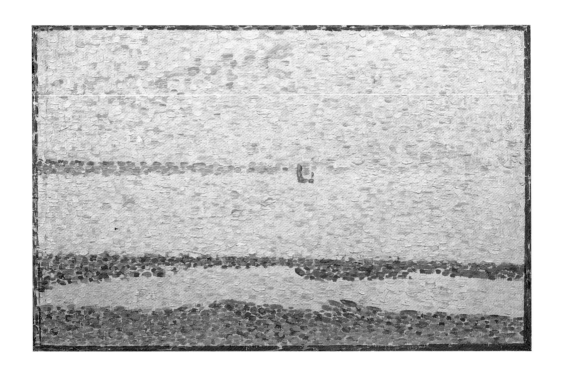

[54]

GEORGES SEURAT

At Gravelines 1890

oil on wood, 16 x 24.5 cm

HISTORY: The artist's mother, Mme Seurat, Paris.
Bought by Samuel Courtauld in 1928 from Alex. Reid & Lefèvre,
London. Courtauld Bequest 1948.

Paul Signac
Paris 1863–1935 Paris

[55]

PAUL SIGNAC

Saint-Tropez 1893

oil on canvas, 19.5 x 28 cm
signed lower left: P. Signac; on reverse: P.S. St Tropez
HISTORY: Bought by Samuel Courtauld in 1928 from Alfred Gold,
Berlin. Courtauld Bequest 1948.

[56]

PAUL SIGNAC

Still Life with Watermelon 1918

pencil and watercolour on paper, 34.4 x 39 cm
signed lower left: P. Signac 1918
HISTORY: Bought by Samuel Courtauld in 1924 from the
Independent Gallery, London. Courtauld Gift 1932.

Henri de Toulouse-Lautrec
Albi 1864-1901 Langon, Gironde

[57]
HENRI DE TOULOUSE-LAUTREC
Jane Avril at the Entrance of the Moulin Rouge 1892
oil and pastel on cardboard, 102 x 55.1 cm
signed lower left (monogram): HTLautrec
HISTORY: Exhibited in Paris, 1893. Murat, Paris. Eugène Blot, Paris
(auctioned in 1900 when unsold, and in 1906). Mancini, Paris;
Prindonoff, Paris; J. Seligmann, New York. Bought by
Samuel Courtauld in 1929 from the Independent Gallery, London.
Courtauld Gift 1932.

In the early 1880s, Toulouse-Lautrec began a systematic study of Parisian lowlife, centred around the brothels, dance halls, and cafés of Montmartre. If he was to be brazenly avant-garde, he had to depict gritty urban experience derived from first-hand observation. For an aristocrat, raised in the seclusion of a provincial family château, it required a period of adjustment. He wrote to his grandmother:

> I am leading a Bohemian life and find it difficult to accustom myself to such a milieu. Indeed one of the chief reasons why I do not feel at my ease on the Butte Montmartre is that I am hampered by a host of sentimental ties which I must absolutely forget if I want to achieve anything.

Consumed by the dissipated life of those he painted, Lautrec died prematurely of alcohol abuse at the age of thirty-six.

The glittering centrepiece in Montmartre of the 1890s was the Moulin Rouge, a dance hall and café which still exists today. Its fame rested on the singers and dancers who performed there. Jane Avril, the model for this painting, was one of its most celebrated stars. An illegitimate daughter of an aristocratic Italian father and a Parisian courtesan, Avril had had a troubled childhood. She lived until 1943, when she died in complete obscurity.

From this painting it is difficult to imagine Avril's provocative performance style, best captured in the famous posters she herself commissioned from Toulouse-Lautrec (fig. 24). In them, she is depicted wriggling and swaying, a bent leg held high. One acquaintance referred to her as a "delirious orchid." However, in the Courtauld painting the mood is surprisingly sombre, as Lautrec documents the duality of the dancer's character. On the stage, Avril was impassioned and frenetic; off-stage, serious and intelligent. Artist and dancer clearly respected each other, and were friends and possibly even lovers, although Avril purportedly told Lautrec she was never in love with him. She certainly became one of his favourite subjects. One cannot but wonder whose overcoat and top hat hang at the left. The artist's, perhaps?

Like many painters of his generation, Lautrec experimented with colour and brush technique, seeking increasingly audacious effects. Here the surface seems to vibrate with a restless tension resulting from Lautrec's use of acidic colour combinations and a complex layering of pastel and oil, nervously worked over each other. D.W.

Fig. 24. Toulouse-Lautrec, *Jane Avril, Jardin de Paris*, 1893, lithograph poster, British Museum, London.

HENRI DE TOULOUSE-LAUTREC
In a Private Room 1899

oil on canvas, 55.1 x 46 cm
signed upper right (monogram): HTLautrec
HISTORY: G. Seré de Rivières, Paris. Georges Bernheim, Paris.
Bought by Samuel Courtauld in 1928 from the Independent Gallery,
London. Courtauld Bequest 1948.

"One has no right to push the cult of the ugly so far," wrote a critic in response to Toulouse-Lautrec's work. No painter before him worked so conscientiously to assault the values of the middle class. How offensive the new subjects—prostitution, drunkenness, debauchery— must have appeared. "The one who's got the biggest cheek of all," another critic wrote, "is Lautrec, that's for certain. He's on his own as a painter of sugar-daddies out on a spree with tarts." Collectively, Lautrec's witty paintings provide a personalized tour of crazy, vulgar, depraved, Parisian lowlife. Not surprisingly, many of his works, including this one, were not exhibited during his lifetime.

In a Private Room was completed just two years before the artist's untimely death. Lautrec had suffered a complete breakdown resulting from years of alcohol abuse and had returned to Paris after convalescing in the countryside. However he was quick to return to the underworld of Montmartre and his earlier habits. Here a celebrated prostitute, Lucy Jourdain, giggles over her champagne (in the narrow flute at the right), while her neighbour, amusingly truncated by the frame, looks away. Perhaps the viewer, whose glass sits in the lower foreground, is really the person paying for the pleasure of Lucy's company, and thus implicated in a sexual transaction. The setting for this picture, Le Rat Mort on the Rue Pigalle at the foot of the Montmartre hill, was a higher class establishment than some. Its private rooms with divans provided an ideal place for revellers to retire to after a masked ball, which probably accounts for Lucy's astonishing attire.

What excitement courses through this painting, despite Lautrec's ailing health. Its garish colours, macabre light effects, voluptuous forms, and frenetic paint application contributed as much to his attack on good taste as the subject matter itself. Surely he understood the import of his own accomplishments. "Everywhere and always," Lautrec said, "ugliness has its beautiful aspects: it is thrilling to discover them where no one else has noticed them." D.W.

[59]

HENRI DE TOULOUSE-LAUTREC
In Bed around 1896

pencil and chalk on paper, 30.3 x 48 cm
signed lower left (monogram): HTLautrec
HISTORY: Gustave Pellet. Claude Sayle. Bought by Samuel Courtauld
in 1922 from the Leicester Galleries, London, 1922.
Courtauld Bequest 1948.

At age fourteen, while convalescing from a broken leg, Lautrec was taught how to draw rapidly from nature, a skill which only improved with time. In this drawing, a network of furious scribbles articulate the sensuous, undulating forms of body and bed with characteristic wit.

During the 1890s Toulouse-Lautrec practically lived in the brothels around the Paris Opéra. There he could observe a secret world, intimately linked to the urban middle class yet publicly rejected by it. Over the years he documented the daily habits of the prostitutes: they chat, eat, play cards, make beds, wash themselves. Strangely enough, few of his drawings portray sexual activities.

Toulouse-Lautrec produced hundreds of "notes" on brothel life. *In Bed* is just one of several such drawings which show a single reclining prostitute, in this case Mlle Popo, the daughter of the madame. Sometimes the woman is depicted asleep; sometimes as here, peering through half-closed eyes. No evidence of the actual location is provided. The drawing, with its rumpled coverlet, and candid, unflattering inclusion of overscaled, protruding legs and feet, might just as well document a lazy, middle-class morning as some post sex-for-money encounter in Paris's seedy underworld. Clearly the artist viewed these women compassionately and sympathized with their way of life. D.W.

Auguste Rodin
Paris 1840–Meudon 1917

[60]

AUGUSTE RODIN

Recumbent Female Nude around 1905

pencil, with rubbing or use of the stump, on paper, 24.8 x 32.5 cm
signed lower right: A Rodin
HISTORY: Given to Sir Robert Witt. Witt Bequest 1952.

Henri Rousseau (called "le Douanier")
Laval 1844-1910 Paris

[61]

HENRI ROUSSEAU

The Toll-Gate perhaps around 1890

oil on canvas, 40.6 x 32.7 cm
signed lower right: H. Rousseau
HISTORY: Wilhelm Uhde, Paris, 1911. Dr. Hartwich, Berlin.
Galerie Flechtheim, Berlin, 1919; sold in 1926 to Samuel Courtauld.
Courtauld Bequest 1948.

Perhaps best known today as a painter of fantastical jungle scenes, Rousseau nevertheless often based his painting on the everyday scenes of suburban Paris. As a collector of tolls on the outskirts of Paris (could the two figures seen in this painting be self-portraits?), he had endless hours to observe the strange collision of urban and rural life at the city gates. Here, modern factory chimneys intrude upon the dense foliage of a nearby hillside.

Rousseau was completely self-taught. He did not even begin painting seriously until age forty, which may account for his often stiff treatment of the human form: here the toll collectors look like cut-outs, and one is perched strangely atop a wall. Such naive idiosyncracies won him few admirers among collectors. However, avant-garde artists like Gauguin, and later Picasso, were fascinated by his flattening of space, bold patterning, and almost dreamlike juxtaposition of forms. Rousseau had the uncanny ability to transform the banal into something incredible. What manner of human or beast are the toll collectors about to encounter in this strange, airless world? D.W.

[62]

PIERRE BONNARD

A Young Woman in an Interior 1906

oil on canvas, 48.9 x 44.5 cm
signed lower right: Bonnard
HISTORY: Acquired by Roger Fry after 1920. Fry Bequest 1934.

PIERRE BONNARD
The Blue Balcony 1910

oil on canvas, 52.5 x 76 cm
signed lower left: Bonnard
HISTORY: Bought by Samuel Courtauld in 1928 from the
Independent Gallery, London, 1928. Courtauld Gift 1932.

[64]

PIERRE BONNARD

Landscape with Olives and a Chapel 1924

oil on canvas, 48 x 61 cm
signed lower centre: Bonnard
HISTORY: Acquired by Roger Fry probably around 1924.
Fry Gift 1934.

[65]

ÉDOUARD VUILLARD

Interior: The Screen around 1909–1910

essence on paper, laid on wood, 35.8 x 23.8 cm
signed lower right: E. Vuillard
HISTORY: Bought by Samuel Courtauld in 1927 from the
Leicester Galleries, London. Courtauld Bequest 1948.

The Courtauld Collection Completed

In 1929, Samuel Courtauld stopped buying paintings on a significant scale. Several factors contributed to this decision, the most obvious being the stock market crash in the autumn of 1929. With an extensive presence in the American market, the income of Courtaulds Ltd. fell from £4 million in 1929 to £100,000 in 1938, while the company's stock lost almost 80 per cent of its value.

An additional factor was the illness of his wife Elizabeth, who died in 1931. She was devoted to music, especially opera, and although we know little about her involvement with the art collection, Samuel Courtauld clearly felt it had been a shared endeavour. The collection's completion was symbolically confirmed when he decided first to give much of it to the new Courtauld Institute of Art, and then to leave the London mansion in which he and his wife had hung their paintings (fig. 25). He turned over its lease to the Courtauld Institute. The new school represented a vigorous challenge and Samuel Courtauld's generous financial support of it may have precluded extensive collecting.

Other Gifts and Bequests

Samuel Courtauld's generosity stimulated other gifts over the years, and the Courtauld Institute of Art has since absorbed several important collections. Lord Lee, principal organizer of the institute, presented a number of paintings, having earlier given his country house, Chequers, to the British nation for the use of the prime minister. In 1941, he gave his collection of Renaissance decorative arts to the Province of Ontario and it is now installed in Toronto's Royal Ontario Museum.[1]

Sir Robert Witt (1872–1952), who also helped found the Courtauld Institute, bequeathed his vast collection of old master prints and drawings to it in 1952. In addition, Witt had also amassed a large collection of photographs of artworks which formed the basis of an important research facility at the institute. Drawings by Boudin and Rodin, originally from Witt's collection, are in this exhibition (cats. 6, 7, 8, 60).

Fig. 25. The Study, Home House, London, with Monet's *Antibes* (cat. 23) over the fireplace. In 1932, Samuel Courtauld turned over his elegant residence designed by Robert Adam to the new Courtauld Institute of Art.

Roger Fry (1866–1934) (fig. 26) also left a number of important nineteenth- and twentieth-century paintings (cats. 62, 64, 66, 78) to the Courtauld Institute. Celebrated as a painter, critic, and art historian, Fry was a major advocate of Cézanne and coined the term "Post-Impressionism" when he arranged an exhibition in 1910 entitled *Manet and the Post-Impressionists* which was devoted to the works of Paul Cézanne, Vincent van Gogh, Paul Gauguin, and Georges Seurat. The exhibition excited a great deal of controversy, particularly around Cézanne. Fry himself depicted one of the galleries in his second Post-Impressionist exhibition of 1912 (fig. 27). As a major intellectual force in the London art world, Fry had considerable influence on Samuel Courtauld's collecting.

A collection equal in importance to Samuel Courtauld's is that bequeathed by Count Antoine Seilern (1901–1978). Modestly titled the Princes Gate Collection, it is especially notable for works by Peter Paul Rubens. Although nineteenth-century pictures form only a small part of the Seilern bequest, some important examples complement Samuel Courtauld's collection (cats. 13, 17, 18, 25, 27, 31, 44, 79, 80). A passion for Cézanne directly links the taste of Courtauld and Seilern. Seilern confessed his lack of interest in much of the nineteenth century:

On the other hand I have lost interest in much of the art of the French eighteenth century—Watteau excepted—and even to some extent in the now so fashionable French nineteenth century—Cézanne excepted. It seems to me now that these certainly very beautiful works of art are concerned primarily with problems of decoration, representation and pure form. They are without doubt most appealing to the eye, and to the mind in so far as it delights in contemplating the development of new representational methods. Only in the work of Cézanne do I still find the solution of these problems exciting.[2]

A.C.

Fig. 26. Roger Fry, *Self-Portrait*, 1928, Courtauld Institute of Art, London.

---

1. Kenneth Clark describes Lee's gift in the early stages of the Second World War: "He had genuine feeling for craftsmanship, and bought admirable pieces of goldsmith's work, which in a panic he presented to Hart House in Toronto in 1941." Clark, *Another Part of the Wood: A Self-Portrait*, London, 1974, p. 206.

2. Antoine Seilern, *Paintings and Drawings of the Continental School other than Flemish and Italian at 56 Princes Gate London SW7*, London, 1961, vol. 1, p. v.

Fig. 27. Roger Fry, *Gallery at the Second Post-Impressionist Exhibition, London*, 1912, Musée d'Orsay, Paris.

André Derain
Chatou 1880–1954 Garches

[66]

ANDRÉ DERAIN

Trees by a Lake, The Park of Carrières Saint-Denis 1909

oil on canvas, 54.1 x 65 cm

HISTORY: Bought by Roger Fry in 1910. Fry Bequest 1934.

Maurice Utrillo
Paris 1883-1955 Dax

[67]

MAURICE UTRILLO
Road at Sannois around 1912
oil on canvas, 55 x 82 cm
signed lower right: Maurice Utrillo
HISTORY: Bought by Samuel Courtauld by 1931 from Libaude, Paris,
through Alex. Reid & Lefèvre, London. Courtauld Gift 1932.

[68]

JEAN-LOUIS FORAIN

Scene at the Court of Assizes around 1909

chalk, watercolour and gouache on paper, 37.9 x 51.5 cm
signed lower right: forain
HISTORY: Bought from the artist by Arthur Tooth & Sons, London;
sold to Samuel Courtauld in 1925. Courtauld Gift 1932.

[69]

JEAN-LOUIS FORAIN

Dancer in the Wings around 1920-1923

watercolour on paper, 45.2 x 29 cm
signed lower right: forain
HISTORY: Bought from the artist by Arthur Tooth & Sons, London;
sold to Samuel Courtauld in 1925. Courtauld Gift 1935.

Amedeo Modigliani
Livorno 1884-1920 Paris

[70]

AMEDEO MODIGLIANI

Nude around 1916

oil on canvas, 92.4 x 59.8 cm
signed upper left: Modigliani
HISTORY: Léopold Zborowski, Paris. C. Zamaron, Paris.
Bought by Samuel Courtauld by 1931 from Léopold Zborowski,
Paris. Courtauld Gift 1932.

Amedeo Modigliani is celebrated for a series of paintings of female nudes made in 1916 and 1917, only four years before his death. Modigliani did not like to work from professional models or friends, but rather chose to paint young women such as housemaids or waitresses as objects of delectation. In the picture in the Courtauld collection, the elongation of the figure and stylized facial features reveal influences that had been at work since early in the artist's career, in particular the impact which Egyptian, African, and Oceanic sculpture had on Modigliani when he first arrived in Paris in 1906.

Nude is typical of Modigliani's sensuous paintings of peach-coloured female flesh set against dark backgrounds. The model's pose is traditional in Western art, yet the artist truncates her legs from the thighs down to call attention to the pelvic area. When Berthe Weill gave Modigliani his first (and last) one-man exhibition in 1917, the police closed it, citing the depiction of pubic hair as obscene. The frank directness of Modigliani's *Nude* no doubt impressed Samuel Courtauld. This picture is an anomaly in his collecting habits, which rarely admitted works associated with twentieth-century modernism. M.P.T.

Aristide Maillol
Banyuls-sur-Mer 1861–1944 Perpignan

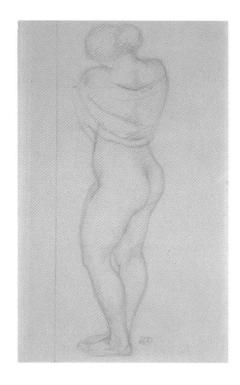

[71]

ARISTIDE MAILLOL

Standing Female Nude around 1918–1923

pencil on paper, 29.4 x 16.9 cm

HISTORY: Bought by Samuel Courtauld in 1924 or 1925
from E. Weyhe, New York. Courtauld Gift 1935.

[72]

ARISTIDE MAILLOL

Woman Undressing around 1919–1920

pencil on paper, 34.9 x 22.1 cm
signed lower centre (monogram): M
HISTORY: Bought by Samuel Courtauld in 1924 or 1925
from E. Weyhe, New York. Courtauld Gift 1935.

[73]
ARISTIDE MAILLOL
Squatting Nude, Viewed from the Rear around 1924
pencil on paper, 30.5 x 21.6 cm
signed lower left: M
HISTORY: Bought by Samuel Courtauld in 1928 from
the Leicester Galleries, London. Courtauld Gift 1935.

[74]
ARISTIDE MAILLOL
Nude Seen from the Back around 1924
pencil on paper, 34 x 23 cm
signed lower right (monogram): M
HISTORY: Bought by Samuel Courtauld in 1928 from
the Leicester Galleries, London. Courtauld Gift 1935.

Henri Matisse
Le Cateau (Picardy) 1869–1954 Nice

[75]

HENRI MATISSE

Seated Woman 1919

pencil on paper, 35.1 x 25.2 cm
signed upper right: Henri-Matisse
HISTORY: Bought by Samuel Courtauld from the Leicester Galleries,
London, 1928. Courtauld Gift 1935.

[76]

HENRI MATISSE

Woman Leaning with Elbows on a Table 1922

chalk and stump on paper, 40.7 x 25.8 cm
signed lower right: Henri-Matisse
HISTORY: Bought by Samuel Courtauld in 1928 from the
Leicester Galleries, London. Courtauld Gift 1935.

[77]

JEAN HIPPOLYTE MARCHAND
Saint-Paul 1921

oil on canvas, 61.5 x 74.5 cm
signed lower right: J. Marchand
HISTORY: Bought by Samuel Courtauld in 1922 from the
Independent Gallery, London. Courtauld Gift 1932.

[78]

JEAN HIPPOLYTE MARCHAND
Still Life with Earthenware Jug, Loaf and Strawberries 1920s
oil on canvas, 61.5 x 53.4 cm
signed lower right: J H Marchand
HISTORY: Roger Fry, London. Fry Bequest 1934.

Oskar Kokoschka
Pöchlarn (Austria) 1886-1980 Montreux

[79]

OSKAR KOKOSCHKA

Market in Tunis 1928-1929

oil on canvas, 86.5 x 129 cm

HISTORY: Acquired by Count Antoine Seilern around 1939-1945.
Seilern Bequest 1978 (Princes Gate Collection).

[80]

OSKAR KOKOSCHKA
Landscape in Scotland (Findhorn River) 1929

oil on canvas, 71 x 91 cm
HISTORY: Acquired by Count Antoine Seilern around 1939-1945 in
London. Seilern Bequest 1978 (Princes Gate Collection).

Acknowledgements

Several dedicated individuals made significant contributions to this publication. Special thanks go to Martha Kelleher, David Wistow and Michael Parke-Taylor for writing informative texts. We are also grateful to Hahn Smith Design for their design of this beautiful catalogue, to Bernice Eisenstein for her sensitive editing, and to Lucie Chevalier for her thoughtful editing of the French edition. Many thanks to Wendy Hebditch and Sarah Head for their effective support.

The entire staff of the Art Gallery of Ontario contributed enormously to the success of the exhibition *The Courtauld Collection* which this book celebrates. In particular, we want to thank our colleagues on the core project team: Norah Farrell, Steven Fong, Rosalind Frydberg, Michelle Koerner, Bruce Maxwell, Suzanne McClimon, Jane Rowland, Heather Sinclair, and David Wistow. Special thanks also to Judith Mastai, Jacqueline Raaflaub, Bruce Borysiuk, Curtis Strilchuk, and Sandra Lawrence. Each of these individuals led a committed team of dedicated professionals. The exhibition was designed by Clarice Kramer-Wolfart and Jim Bourke. Installation of the exhibition was the responsibility of Myron Jones, George Bartosik, Bryan Groombridge and their exceptionally skilled preparation team.

The experience of working with the extraordinary collection of the Courtauld Gallery would not have been possible without the efforts of the AGO director, Maxwell L. Anderson. The advice and support offered by him and by the chief curator, Matthew Teitelbaum, have been crucial throughout.

Alan Chong
CURATOR OF EUROPEAN ART

Linda Milrod
PROJECT DIRECTOR
THE COURTAULD COLLECTION

Selected Bibliography

This publication draws upon the books listed below, as well as from the catalogues raisonné of individual artists. Most of the paintings included in this exhibition are fully catalogued in John House, *Impressionism for England: Samuel Courtauld as Patron and Collector*, London, 1994.

Boggs, Jean Sutherland, et al. *Degas*. Exhibition catalogue, Grand Palais, Paris; National Gallery of Canada, Ottawa; Metropolitan Museum of Art, New York. 1988-1989.

Brettell, Richard, et al. *A Day in the Country: Impressionism and the French Landscape*. Exhibition catalogue, Los Angeles County Museum of Art; Art Institute of Chicago; Grand Palais, Paris. 1984-1985.

Cachin, Françoise and Joseph Rishel, et al. *Cézanne*. Exhibition catalogue, Grand Palais, Paris; Tate Gallery, London; Philadelphia Museum of Art. 1995-1996.

Clark, T. J. *The Painting of Modern Life: Paris in the Art of Manet and his Followers*. New York, 1985.

Collins, Bradford R., ed. *12 Views of Manet's Bar*. Princeton, 1996.

Cooper, Douglas. *The Courtauld Collection: A Catalogue and Introduction*. London, 1954.

Frèches-Thory, C., et al. *Toulouse-Lautrec*. Exhibition catalogue, Hayward Gallery, London; Grand Palais, Paris. 1991-1992.

Fried, Michael. *Manet's Modernism, or, The Face of Painting in the 1860s*. Chicago, 1996.

Herbert, Robert. *Impressionism: Art, Leisure, and Parisian Society*. New Haven, 1988.

———, et al. *Seurat*. Exhibition catalogue, Grand Palais, Paris; Metropolitan Museum of Art, New York. 1991.

House, John. *Monet: Nature into Art*. New Haven, 1986.

Moffett, Charles, et al. *The New Painting: Impressionism 1874-1886*. Exhibition catalogue, National Gallery of Art, Washington; Fine Arts Museums of San Francisco. 1986.

Pissarro, Joachim. *Monet and the Mediterranean*. Exhibition catalogue, Kimbell Art Museum, Fort Worth; Brooklyn Museum of Art. 1997-1998.

Rewald, John. *The History of Impressionism*. 4th ed. New York, 1973.

Shiff, R. L. *Cézanne and the End of Impressionism: A Study of the Theory, Technique and Critical Evaluation of Modern Art*. Chicago, 1984.

Wilson Barreau, Juliet. *The Hidden Face of Manet: An Investigation of the Artist's Working Processes*. Exhibition catalogue, Courtauld Institute Galleries, London, 1986. [published in *Burlington Magazine* 128 (1986)]

Index of Artists

Editor: Bernice Eisenstein
Editor, French edition: Lucie Chevalier
Translator: André Bernier
Design: Hahn Smith Design, Toronto
Typeset in Bembo and Avenir by Richard Hunt, Archetype
Printed in Canada by Bowne of Toronto
on Quintessence Dull

Photo Credits
All photographs are courtesy of the owner of the work
of art, with the following exceptions:
Fig. 1, p. 18: Courtaulds plc
Fig. 3, p. 19: Photograph by Dennis Gilbert,
copyright Dennis Gilbert/VIEW
Fig. 10, p. 39: Country Life Picture Library
Fig. 25, p. 124: Country Life Picture Library